INDIA IMPRESSIONS

INDIA IMPRESSIONS

WITH SOME NOTES OF CEYLON DURING A WINTER TOUR, 1906-7

WALTER CRANE

GYAN

Published by

Gyan Publishing House
5, Ansari Road
Daryaganj, New Delhi-110002
Phone: 011-47034999, 9811692060
E-mail: books@gyanbooks.com

Distribution Network
gyanbooks.com
India, USA, Canada, UK, Australia, France

ISBN: 978-81-212-8724-1 (PB)
First Published, 1907

2nd Impression 2023

Printed at: Gyan Press, Delhi.

INDIA IMPRESSIONS
Author: Walter Crane

INDIA IMPRESSIONS

THE MAUIKARNIKÁ GHÁT
BENARES

INDIA IMPRESSIONS

WITH SOME NOTES OF CEYLON DURING A WINTER TOUR, 1906-7 BY WALTER CRANE, R.W.S. WITH A FRONTISPIECE AND NUMEROUS OTHER ILLUSTRATIONS FROM SKETCHES BY THE AUTHOR

LONDON: METHUEN & CO.
36, ESSEX STREET, STRAND

First Published in 1907

TO MY WIFE
MY TRAVELLING COMPANION
ON THIS TOUR, AND TO WHOM
THE PROJECT WAS DUE, I
NOW INSCRIBE ITS RECORD

PREFACE

ALTHOUGH many books descriptive of India and Indian life have recently appeared, even a short visit to that wonderful country presents so extraordinary a series of spectacles to the European, especially to one seeing the East for the first time, that it occurred to me that a few notes and fresh impressions from an artist's point of view, accompanied by sketches made on the spot, as well as illustrations of the lighter side of travel, might not be without interest to the public.

Even apart from the enormous artistic interest and architectural splendours of India, which are so rich and abundant that one feels that hundreds of drawings would be necessary to give any adequate idea of their beauty, there is the human interest of these vast populations, among whom so many streams of race, language and religion are found, not to speak of the problems of government and administration they present.

I cannot claim to have had any special facilities in seeing the country—no more at least than might be at the command of an ordinary English tourist, and have trusted chiefly to what powers of observation I may possess in describing the various cities visited, and the districts traversed, and I offer these notes strictly as personal impressions.

Owing to ever increasing facilities of travel, the East is, in a sense, drawn nearer to the West, or, rather the West to the East, but nothing strikes the traveller so much as the apparently vast gulf dividing the dark-skinned races from the white—a gulf deeper and wider than the oceans.

I mean the profound differences in ideas, in religion, in sentiment, in life, habit and custom. Western influence where even it has had any apparent effect—apart from commercial enterprise—seems to be but a thin veneer, and it is a constant wonder how the British should have been able to acquire and maintain their grasp over this vast peninsular, and to hold the balance between antagonistic races and creeds so long.

But it is not a comfortable thought for an Englishman, loving freedom, and accustomed to the principles of popular and representative government at home, to realise that this vast empire is held under the strictest autocratic system; and that the national aspirations that are now beginning to make themselves heard and felt should be entirely ignored, and the voice of native feeling sternly suppressed.

One can only hope that the great British people will take more trouble to study and understand their great Dependency, and not be prevented by official explanations from making independent inquiries and observations for themselves, and finally to "be just and fear not."

If, however, in any way and from any point of view, these impressions may serve, in however slight a degree, to increase the interest of my own countrymen and women in India, I shall be very glad.

WALTER CRANE

KENSINGTON, *July* 1907

CONTENTS

LIST OF ILLUSTRATIONS IN THE TEXT

LIST OF PLATES

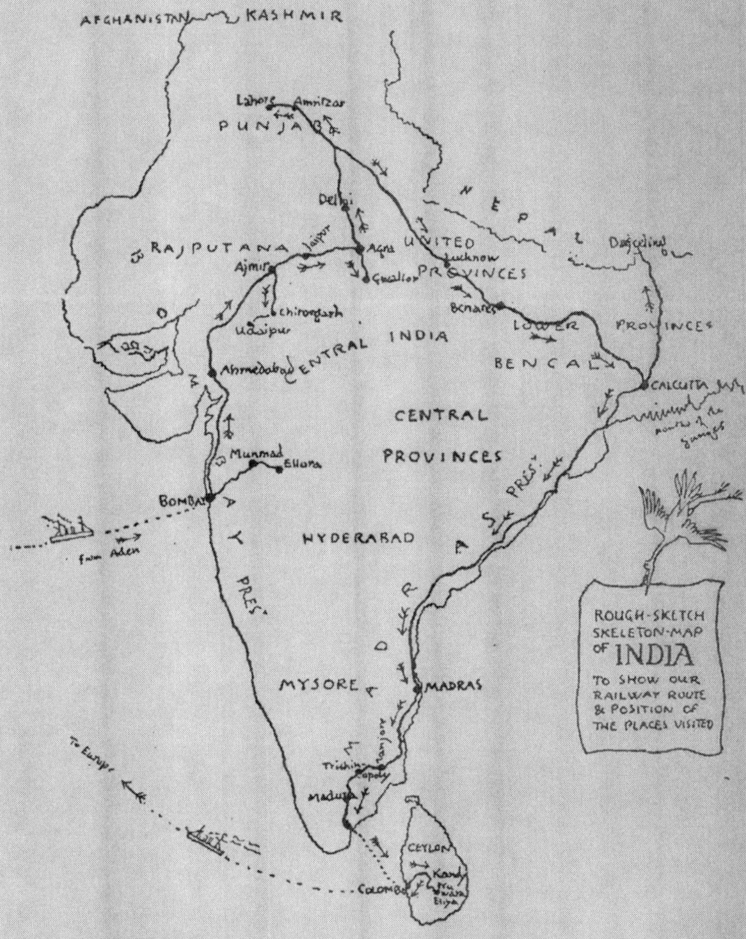
AFGHANISTAN
KASHMIR
Lahore
Amritzar
PUNJAB
NEPAL
Delhi
RAJPUTANA
Jaipur
Agra
UNITED PROVINCES
Lucknow
Ajmir
Gwalior
Darjeeling
Chitorgarh
Udaipur
Benares
LOWER PROVINCES
CENTRAL INDIA
BENGAL
Ahmedabad
CALCUTTA
CENTRAL PROVINCES
Munmad
Ellora
BOMBAY
from Aden
HYDERABAD
PRES.
MADRAS
MYSORE
To Europe
Trichinopoly
Tanjore
Madura
CEYLON
Kandy
Nuwara Eliya
COLOMBO
ROUGH-SKETCH SKELETON-MAP OF INDIA TO SHOW OUR RAILWAY ROUTE & POSITION OF THE PLACES VISITED

INDIA IMPRESSIONS

CHAPTER I

THE VOYAGE

A VISIT to India and the East had long been a cherished but somewhat vague dream with us. It seemed a far cry, and to make a break of a few months in the midst of the occupations of a busy life is always a difficult matter. The impossible, however, became in course of time possible, and even practicable. Inquiries as to ways and means had the effect of clearing our path; and having the *will*, the *way* was soon discovered.

"Only sixteen days to Bombay!" our Indian friends in London told us, and they were always urging us to go and see their wonderful country for ourselves. Mr Romesh Dutt and Dr Mulich had been visitors at our house. The former had presented his interesting translation of the "Ramayana," illustrated by Miss Hardy, to my wife. Besides these we had from time to time made the acquaintance of several native gentlemen in London who were reading for the Indian Bar. They came and went, but all were earnest in their hope that we should visit India, and I think that they had discovered our sympathies were with those of their countrymen in their aspirations to participate in the administration of the affairs of their own country.

The decisive step of booking our passage was at last taken in the summer of 1906, and the 19th day of November following saw us *en route* for Marseilles, where we committed ourselves to the care of the Messageries Maritime, and embarked on the S.S. "La Nera" in due course, putting to sea on Wednesday, the 21st November.

It was a lovely bright afternoon as we left the port, the southern sunshine flooding everything in golden light. It is a wonderful moment when the ship casts off. The great liner, which had seemed a part of the land itself while the stream of passengers passed up the gangways, and their baggage after them, begins to throb with life and movement—to tremble, as it were, with expectation of departure. As a swimmer about to take the water casts off all impedimenta, so the ship casts off her cables and all that links her to the shore, and glides off into the great blue deep, breasting the waves of the vast open sea. Incredibly fast as the engines beat the solid land fades away. The domes and towers and chimneys silhouetted against the bright sky, the people on the quays, the ships riding at anchor, the tossing harbour buoys, the small sailing craft flitting about, all are rolled by as on the canvas of a moving diorama, as the steamer clears the port, and all detail becomes merged and lost under the bold main outlines of the rocky coast, or the dim shapes of the distant mountains.

As the long shining wake increases astern and

the coast recedes, those nautical camp-followers the gulls, which have pursued the ship from the harbour, begin to diminish their numbers, though

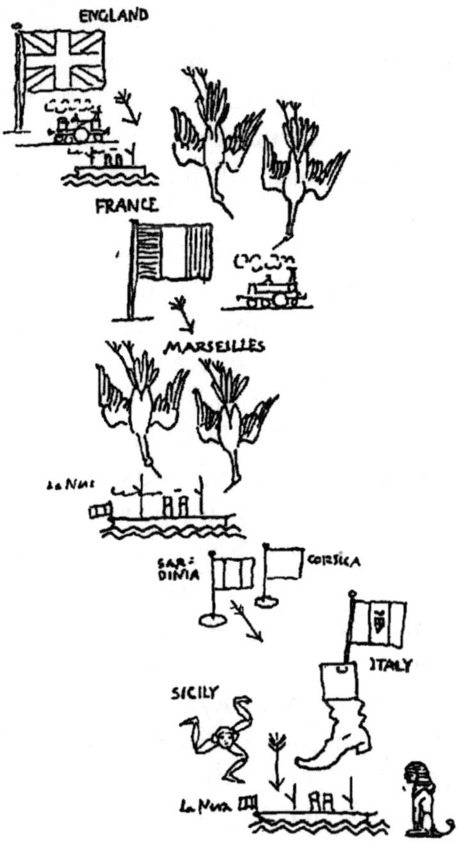

LONDON TO PORT SAID, A HIEROGLYPHIC OF OUR VOYAGE

they wing a long way out to sea, attracted by the crumbs which occasionally fall from the region of the cook's galley.

A glorious sunset inaugurated our first night at sea—of the order of the Golden Fleece, as it might be called—a distinct type, when in a windless sky a large field of delicate fleecy cirrus cloud spreads in a level field from west to east, and as the sun sinks its under edges are lighted up by golden light, changing to orange, scarlet, and crimson, when he disappears beneath the horizon. So our voyage began propitiously, and with a smooth sea. Early the next morning we passed through the Straits of Bonifazio, between Corsica and Sardinia, the coasts of which we had a glimpse of through our port-hole, and on the morning of the third day, after a little tossing, we sighted Sicily, passing Scylla and Charybdis at the entrance of the straits, and close to Messina. Etna soon came into view, its summit covered with a crown of snow (as we had seen it on our visit to Taormina in 1904).

The Calabrian coast, too, was very interesting, the mountains of striking form, and the lines very varied all along to Cape Spartivento—the toe of the boot-shaped continent of Italy. We could see the little white towns along the coast and among the hills, and the monasteries perched high upon crags. Etna gradually faded away, like a vision, beyond the dark blue edge of the sea, and almost immediately after passing the cape we encountered a strong easterly wind from the Adriatic, which met the Mediterranean here.

At sunset there were huge banks of grey clouds of fantastic shapes rising like high wooded islands, but we had moonlight on the waters every night.

Those grey banks of cloud, however, were ominous, and by November the 24th the weather grew so rough that the "fiddle-strings" became necessary on the tables in the dining-saloon, where the attendance, too, grew distinctly thinner. Towards evening we sighted the cliffs of Crete (Candia), the fissured, mountainous, and dangerous-looking coast plainly visible in the sunlight, though a bank of cloud covered the summits of the island.

After much tossing and rolling through another day and night the lights of Port Said were sighted about four o'clock on the morning of November 26. There was a powerful search-light from the light-house. We got into harbour about 5.30, and the coaling began. It was a weird scene. Six black lighters were hauled alongside our steamer, three on the port bow and three on the starboard, and boats crowded to the water's edge with coolies in long ragged garments and turbans, mostly of a dusky red and blue, the colours shining through the coal dust which darkened their naturally swarthy visages and forms. As these crowded boats approached with their weird passengers, one had an irresistible suggestion of Charon ferrying lost souls across the Styx—there was generally only one pair of oars, as the distance to the steamer from the wharf was very short. Well, these were our coal-slaves, upon whose cheap labour the speed of our steamers depends quite as much as on their own engines, one felt. From the boats they scrambled into the lighters—some shovelled up the coal into hand baskets of matting which others lifted on to their shoulders and carried across a narrow plank into the ship, forming a weird line of black figures silhouetted against the shining water. The coolies worked hard and fast in a black mist of coal dust and kept up a continual hubbub of cries in Arabic and other strange tongues which added to the weirdness of the scene.

Port Said looked very new and flimsy, and was

COALING AT PORT SAID—AND AFTER!

hopelessly vulgarised by flaming posters and advertisements of Western origin both in French and English. Boats swarmed round the ship's side, and swarthy eager-eyed hotel touts came aboard in Fez caps, as well as a motley crowd of traders, Egyptian conjurers, and European musicians who played the latest popular waltzes. We were glad to escape the coal dust and go ashore, where an intelligent but probably not too scrupulous Egyptian guide undertook to show us everything, and we went with him round the town, passing through the market crowded with the picturesque life of the

SPOILING THE EGYPTIANS? OR BEING DESPOILED BY THEM!

SENSATION IN SOLAR TOPIS

East, which indeed showed itself everywhere through the thin veneer of modern European commercialism. A venerable-looking prophet swept the streets, and, of course, there were plenty of street arabs ready to turn "cart-wheels" or anything that would turn a more or less honest penny in their direction, and the cry of "Backsheesh" was raised on the slightest provocation. Our guide took us into a small Mohammedan mosque, modern, but, of course, strictly according to the traditional plan and oriented towards Mecca. We had to put on loose canvas shoes over our own shoes to enter the sacred precincts, and our guide gave us a long exposition of the necessary ablutions to be performed by the faithful before and after prayers, and showed us the water tank fitted with taps, at one of which a devotee was busy having his wash.

The bazaar bristled with European goods, and topis and cigarettes were much in evidence, though there were some charming Egyptian fabrics in the form of scarves brocaded with patterns in gold or silver thread or black on white fine linen.

On the whitewashed walls of some of the houses I noticed some primitive paintings in distemper, apparently representing camels, travellers, and palm-trees, done in profile. They were carried horizontally across the front of the houses as a sort of frieze, and were curiously suggestive in a child-like way of a survival of the ancient Egyptian method of decorating. Our guide said that they indicated that the dweller in the house had visited Mecca. Returning to "La Nera" we found her indeed blacker than she was painted, as everything on board was covered with a fine coal dust, which the energy of the crew with copious hose-pipes eventually got rid of. The harbour of Port Said is always busy, many liners and transports coming and going, war vessels of various nationalities lying at anchor, boats plying to and fro, and young, lithe, brown-skinned natives on the quays, ready to dive for silver pieces, crouching shivering on the edge of the wharf, or in a boat, and crying in an almost continuous monotone, "à la mer," "à la mer," "à la mer," until the hoped-for small coin is thrown into the water, when they adroitly dive and intercept it as it falls turning and glittering in the water, and reappear with it in their mouths, which soon open for more.

We started again at 12.30 for Suez, entering the

THE SUEZ CANAL

canal. Our steamer was stopped at the first village to allow two steamers to pass—the "Clan Campbell" of Glasgow and the "Herefordshire" of Liverpool.

The weather was quite cool and cloudy and it turned out a showery afternoon. Flocks of pelicans were seen on the waters of the wide shallow lakes we passed. There was a stormy sunset, and there was lightning after nightfall, but later the moon shone brightly, falling on the wan sand of the banks, which had quite the effect of snow under its clear cold light.

The steamer moved slowly through the canal at about the rate of five knots. A passenger was landed at Ismailia, after which we entered the bitter lakes, and next morning we were within fifteen miles from Suez, but our steamer had to stop owing to a transport ship having got aground ahead of us. A German steamer was close behind us, and while waiting many of the passengers landed and roamed about on the desert sand. It was not long, however, before the transport was got off, and she presently passed us, a huge white steamer named the "Rena," crowded with English "Tommies" homeward bound.

The passage of the Suez Canal is very interesting and comes as a welcome relief after tossing on the open sea out of sight of land. The long level lines of the sandy desert have a reposeful effect, but fine ranges of mountains are often seen beyond, and the desert is frequently varied with the

> "strip of herbage strown"

embroidered with palm-trees, and these elements of Egyptian landscape steeped in the translucent atmosphere are relieved by striking bronze-coloured figures in blue robes and swarthy Arabs in white in the foreground on the sand-banks, or an occasional string of camels.

We reached Suez about midday and anchored off the town. The Consul's tug paid us a visit, and our vessel was soon surrounded by a small fleet of picturesque craft with lateen sails, and gunwales painted with eyes, and in the semblance of quaint fish in bands of green and white, manned by swarthy Arabs and Egyptians. These brought cargo and provisions to be hoisted on board, and the process took an hour or two, but in the afternoon we steamed away again and entered the Red Sea.

The weather grew perceptibly warmer, but was still not oppressive, and there was a cool breeze in the evening. There was a beautiful roseate light at afterglow on the eastern shore, where Mount Sinai was pointed out, and the well of Moses, and the traditional place of the Israelites' passage of the Red Sea. The sun set in gold and purple behind a bold range of craggy mountains on our starboard side, and a splendid moonlight night succeeded, the moon nearly at full.

On the morning of the 28th November we passed "The Brothers" lightships to starboard, and the next day we were out of sight of land, with a pleasant breeze under the double awnings of the upper deck, enjoying the best summer weather, which we should think ourselves lucky to have in England. The Red Sea was really as blue as the Mediterranean, though of course subject to changes according to the sky, which turned to a wonderful clear greenish gold after sunset, powdered with small dark clouds which floated across it; a violet flush above the gold blending it into the deep blue of the upper sky, the small floating clouds against it showing ashy grey, while against the gold of the afterglow they looked nearly black, the sea being of a rather cold metallic blue. The serene weather and the splendour of the moonlit nights continued, but the temperature rose considerably, reaching 88° Fahr. in our cabin, which was on the starboard side of the ship. It is as well to remember that port side cabins are cooler for the outward voyage, and those on the starboard side for the homeward voyage, as going eastwards the heat of the sun falls on the starboard side necessarily for the greater part of the day, while going westwards of course the reverse is the case. This applies more particularly to the Red Sea.

On November 30th we passed the island of

THE PASSAGE OF THE RED SEA
(Therm: 88° or so!)

Jubbelteer, on which was a lighthouse, and later, "The Twelve Apostles," a series of rocky volcanic-looking islands of bold and angular outline, and apparently barren. Sea-birds, however, were seen with black and white bodies and brown wings flying close to the water.

On December the 1st we passed Mocha, of coffee celebrity, and the island of Perrim, where there are lighthouses and signal stations, but, like the other islands we had seen, otherwise desolate in the extreme. Later the Arabian coast came into view and the sea was dotted with the sails of Arab dhows. The coast as we approached Aden showed volcanic-looking mountains, striking in form and bold in outline, with stretches of sand and rock between. Aden was reached about 2 P.M., a school of dolphins playing about the ship as if to welcome our arrival.

Aden looked a queer uninviting place, baked dry by the sun—a cluster of temporary and barrack-like buildings huddled together anyhow along the rocky coast, with never a tree to be seen; the ragged, precipitous, barren edges of extinct volcanoes forming a background to the red-roofed barracks and bungalows.

Several large white warships lay at anchor in the harbour, and lent a touch of gay colour by being decked with strings of bunting from stem to stern in honour of our Queen Alexandra's birthday. A German liner got in just before us and we saw the coal lighters being rowed up to her. "La Nera" coaled here also, but it was a less grimy proceeding than at Port Said, as the coal was in sacks. The type of coolies, too, was very different, and there were many African negroes (Soumalis) among them, whose skins could hardly be made blacker than they were by nature. In addition to its cluster of coaling lighters, our vessel, now at anchor, was soon surrounded by boats filled with natives who swarmed round the gangways, and soon invaded the ship—a crowd of Soumali traders offering ostrich feathers and feather fans (of a European look), ostrich eggs, wicker bottle-shaped baskets, shell necklaces, and amber beads, who drove their trade amongst the passengers on deck, whilst others endeavoured to catch their eyes from the boats. Thin, lithe young natives with fuzzy hair were very numerous, and some had dyed their hair red, which had a grotesque effect with the black skin. I noted a strange contrast in the same boat, too, which contained two natives, one of whom wore a sort of large-checked suit of pyjamas with his mop of red-dyed hair, while his companion had his head clean shaved with "nodings on"! Some natives seemed to have used face powder—at

IN THE SAME BOAT—A CONTRAST AT ADEN

any rate had smeared some kind of whitening over their countenances with ghastly effect.

The scene was a strange one altogether. The crowd of Europeans on deck, in which nearly every nationality was represented, mostly clad in topis and white garments, the black traders moving about them; the swarm of boats at the sides of the vessel full of bright spots of colour—scarlet turbans, white, orange, yellow, and purple in the costumes—swaying on the turquoise-coloured sea; brown-backed gulls flapping over the water and kites hovering over the harbour; and all steeped in the bright sunshine of the East. Many of the passengers went ashore in the native boats, but the scene seemed more amusing from the ship and we remained on deck.

Aden itself looked more interesting at night, with bright lights here and there on the shore and on the ships, and the rising moon translated everything into terms of mystery and romance.

I watched an Arab dhow set sail. It is one of the most beautiful of sailing vessels, and has a high old-fashioned poop—the line of the gunwale making a fine curve from stem to stern—a main-mast with a big lateen sail, two jibs on a short bowsprit, and a secondary smaller mast astern. The sun set behind the Arabian coast, the jagged peaks of which we had previously passed. The coaling did not finish till nightfall. The coolies seemed to undertake all the mechanical arrangements for the work, fixing the hauling gear and the necessary ropes and planks, and often in the process seeming to hang on to the ship with little more than their eyelids. When they pulled a rope together the cry to keep time sounded like "Leesah!" or "Leeshah!" with emphasis on the first syllable.

The coaling finished, and the curious swarm of native life that had surrounded us departed, "La Nera" weighed anchor and pursued her course eastwards, skirting the rocky coast bathed in the moonlight as she made for the open Arabian Sea.

The next day in the early morning we had sight of some flying-fish. They have almost the appearance of swallows at a distance, especially when seen against the light, but, glancing, as they leap out of the water, to disappear into it again very quickly, they flash in the sun like silver.

The Arabian coast was still faintly visible towards the north, but gradually faded from view. The pleasant light breeze continued and it was not nearly so hot as in the Red Sea, in fact quite pleasant either on deck or below—especially with a "windle" fixed to the cabin port.

We had made an interesting acquaintance on board, a French gentleman who knew India well and who was on his way to revisit that country, intending to join an English friend there on a shooting expedition. He was an old sportsman and had shot big game in Tibet. He united the keenness and experience of a sportsman with literary tastes and a love of history and archæology. This gentleman introduced us to "the green ray," a phenomenon peculiar to the Eastern seas, I believe. Just at the moment when the sun disappears beneath the horizon there is the appearance of a vivid green spark flashing like a gem which seems to detach itself from the glowing orb and fly upward, instantly disappearing in the reddening haze. We witnessed this on several occasions, but in order to see it a clear sunset is absolutely necessary—that is to say that one must be able to see the sun sink below the horizon clear of cloud. The lovely moonlight nights continued, the moon being now ahead, and the apparent goal of the vessel's course. One night, however, was disturbed by the steamer stopping in mid-ocean. One gets so accustomed to the throb of the engines on board a steamer that its sudden cessation is quite startling. Passengers clustered near the engine-room to learn the cause, which turned out to be something wrong with "a washer" which affected the movement of the shaft. After about three hours this was repaired and the "Nera" continued her course. She generally made about 300 miles in the twenty-four hours.

Incidents in the Indian Ocean were few and far between. Flying-fish were to be seen, but only in

SOME TYPES AMONG OUR FELLOW PASSENGERS

the early morning as a rule; a whale was noticed spouting, and two sharks were sighted. I saw, too, a large turtle turn over close to the ship's side, but such sights very occasionally varied the wide sea-scape, and many were glad to turn to deck games or bridge for diversion, if they could not find it in books, or in observing their fellow passengers.

Certainly amongst these latter there was no want of interest or variety; they were quite an international group, and included English and Anglo-Indians returning after leave of absence in Europe to take up their official duties, civil or military, on new appointments with their wives and families; a large proportion of French (it being a French steamer); then there were Portuguese and Dutch (going out to Australia), Germans and Canadians, Armenians from Rangoon, and Indians from Bombay; several Armenian priests also, probably missionaries; there were negroes and Arabs in the fo'castle, and among the second-class passengers a characteristic group of English workmen—foremen engineers and navvies. They were bound for Bombay, having been engaged to direct coolie labour on new and extensive docks at that port, their contract being for three years, and their passage paid. I think they got very tired of doing nothing and did not feel quite happy with the French dinners, although the heaviest man of the party made it a rule to devour everything that was set before him, taking Saint Paul's advice, and "asking no questions." I think all the ages of man—and woman—were represented on board, including more than one infant "mewling and puling in its nurse's arms." A little sample of the big world chipped off and sent adrift on the ocean—a ship of life, not without its enigmas, its little ironies and uncertainties, tossed upon the very type of uncertainty—the sea.

A ship, however, is a castle of indolence as far as the passengers are concerned, though the crew, I suspect, would tell a very different story, as, apart from the severe work of the engineers and stokers, their work never seems at an end, and it is only by constant washing, scrubbing, and sweeping that a steamer can be kept decently clean and habitable.

To break the monotony of the five days' voyage on the Indian Ocean a concert was got up by an energetic young lady and her friends. They went round the ship to discover what hidden musical or histrionic talent might be concealed under the more or less disguised personalities of the passengers, and they succeeded in drawing out enough for an evening's entertainment on the saloon deck, which was picturesquely draped with bunting for the occasion, and a piano was wheeled into position. Various songs were given, and a French princess, who was among the passengers, recited. The young lady who had been the leading spirit in organising the concert herself gave some charming songs which she accompanied on a guitar, and a pretty song in Japanese costume and umbrella from "The Geisha," I think, with much spirit. The proceeds went to the benefit of the orphans of the Messageries Maritimes sailors.

After this violent excitement the days passed as days do at sea, the fine weather continuing with delightful monotony. The fresh easterly breeze was strong enough to fleck the blue plain with "white horses," yet not cause any trying movement of the vessel, which ploughed steadily through the waves, driving the spray from its bows, and causing dancing rainbows on the foamy crests as they rebounded from the ship's side. The sun rising in clear glory from the sea, disappeared each evening in tranquil splendour, showing the green ray, and the deep red along the horizon in the west afterwards, over the dark blue sea. The dark blue above and the illuminated sky between, recalled the favourite effect in Japanese prints by Hiroshigi, and at the same time testified to its truth.

But all things have an end, even ocean voyages, and about four o'clock on the morning of Friday, December the 7th, our steamer slowed down and took on board the pilot, and we, cautiously steering past mysterious islands under the dawn, finally cast anchor in Bombay harbour.

CHAPTER II

BOMBAY AND THE CAVES OF ELLORA

THE first impression of Bombay from the sea is perhaps a little disappointing from the pictorial point of view. The town spreads along the low flat coast, lined with long quays without any great domes or conspicuous noble buildings. One is aware of wharves and factory chimneys, and even the palms and gardens of Malabar Hill, and blue mountains inland do not altogether mitigate the commercial and industrial aspects of the place; but the light and colour of the East fuse all sorts of incongruities, and the feeling of touching a strange land and of setting foot for the first time in India is sufficiently exciting to throw a sort of glamour over everything.

The steamers cannot disembark their passengers at the quays, so they have to be landed in boats which cluster about the sides of the big liner. The official tug comes alongside first, and the official visit is paid. We were due the evening before, and inquiries as to the why and wherefore of the delay had to be satisfied. Busy agents and eager hotel touts come on board, and all is bustle and preparation for landing.

Our Indian friend had been unexpectedly called away and was unable to meet us, but he committed us to the care of other friends at Bombay. We landed, however, with our friend the French explorer, with all our baggage, in a native boat, and by dint of a ragged lateen sail and oars plied by a swarthy, wild-looking crew, soon reached the quay, where a crowd of coolies waited to spring upon our belongings.

Our French friend spoke Hindustanee fluently,

LANDING AT BOMBAY

fortunately for us; and amid the clamour of tongues which surrounded us, was able to arrange for an ox-cart to take our united baggage to the Custom-House, where, after an interview with some languid English officials clad in white drill and topis, having nothing contraband, we were duly passed, though our friend, possessing firearms, was delayed longer, and of course had to pay. The Bombay ox-carts are two-wheeled with high sides of timber, forming a square open lattice, and drawn by a pair of oxen.

Committing our worldly goods to this delightful prehistoric vehicle, we took a carriage—a little, one-horse, open victoria, which is the street cab of Bombay, and similar to those in use in the towns of Italy—and drove to the Taj-Mahal Hotel, a vast, new, modern caravanserai—which, however, was quite full, so we went on to the old-established "Watson's" on the Esplanade, where we got a good

AWAITING THE CUSTOMS—BOMBAY

room with a balcony and a view. There was also a pleasant covered terrace, or verandah, extending the whole length of the building, which on the north side, always in shade, faced a garden green with well-watered lawns and thickly planted with umbrageous mango and banyan trees, amid which the ubiquitous crows of India (resembling our hooded crow) kept up a continual cawing chorus as they flitted about, now swooping down on some ill-considered trifle in the street, or perching expectantly about the hotel precincts, on the look-out for scattered crumbs. Great brown kites hovered in the air, forming a second line of watchful but silent scavengers. The terrace also commanded a view of the street with all its varied

STREET PERFORMERS—BOMBAY

types in costume, race, and colour and character. The prosperous, sleek Parsee merchant in his curious shiny, sloping high hat, long black alpaca or white tunic, and loose white nether garments and umbrella; Europeans in white drill and grey or white pith helmets, which gave a superficial family likeness to all who wore them; native servants, Hindu, Portuguese, and half-caste, in every variety of turban and costume, sitting or standing about in groups, waiting to be hired; wandering minstrels, dancing women, and jugglers and tumblers trying to catch the eye—and the small change—of the traveller; men with tom-toms and performing monkeys water-carriers with their dripping goat-skin slung at their side, coolies and coolie women constantly passing to and fro from the quays, bearing their burdens on their heads; the bearer and the ayah in charge of faired-haired English children, passing in and out of the gardens; the British soldier in khaki, and the native policeman in blue with a flat yellow cap. These and such as these were the prevailing types in the scene from the hotel balcony, from whence, also, we could see the tram-cars, drawn by horses in big white topis, trailing up and down the Esplanade, while motors flashed by, and smart European ladies drove in their dog-carts. Beyond the trees of the garden rose a modern clock-tower which told the burning hours in the familiar Westminster chimes.

The modern British buildings of Bombay would probably in newspaper language be described as "handsome." There were many showy and pretentious structures in a sort of Italian Gothic style, but they looked imported, and were decidedly out of place in a country which possesses such magnificent specimens of architecture of its own growth—as one might say. The many balconied and shuttered fronts, with projecting stories, the ridge-tiled roofs and plastered walls that we saw in the older quarters of the town seemed, as types of dwelling-houses at least, much more suitable and characteristic, and such types would surely be capable of adaptation to modern requirements. The Crawford Market is one of the sights of Bombay. Outside, with its steep roofs, belfry, and projecting eaves it has a rather English Gothic look, but inside the scene is entirely oriental, crowded with natives in all sorts of colours, moving among fish, fruit, grain, and provisions of all kinds, buying and selling amid a clamour of tongues—a busy scene of colour and variety, in a symphony of smells, dominated by that of the smoke of joss-sticks kept burning at some of the stalls as well as a suspicion of opium, which pervades all the native quarters in Indian cities. There is a sort of court or garden enclosed by the buildings, and here the live stock is kept—all sorts of birds and animals.

A drive through the native bazaar of Bombay is a revelation. The carriage works its way with difficulty through the narrow, irregular street, crowded with natives in every variety of costume (or next to no costume), forming a wonderful moving pattern of brilliant colour, punctuated by swarthy faces, gleaming eyes, and white teeth. Shops of every kind line each side of the way, and these are rather dark and cavernous openings, shaded by awnings and divided by posts or carved pillars on the lowest story, but raised from the level of the streets by low platforms which serve the purposes of counter and working bench to the native merchant or craftsman who squats upon it, and often unites the two functions in his own person. He generally carries on his work in the presence of his whole family, apparently. All ages and sexes crowd in and about the shops, carrying on a perpetual conversazione, and the bazaar literally swarms with dusky, turbaned faces, varied by the deep red sari of the Hindu women, with their glittering armlets and anklets, or the veiled Mohammedan in her—well, pyjamas!

The older house fronts above the shops were often rich with carving and colour, the upper stories being generally supported over the open shop by four columns. It reminded one of the arrangement of a mediæval street, as also in its general aspect, the shops being mostly workshops; and, as in the old days in Europe, could be seen different crafts in full operation, while the finished products of each were displayed for sale. There were tailors stitching away at garments, coppersmiths hammering their metal into shape, leather workers, jewellers, cook-shops, and many more, the little dark shops in most cases being crowded with other figures besides those of the workers—each like a miniature stage of life with an abundance of drama going on in all. The whole bazaar, too, was gay with colour—white, green, red, orange, yellow, and purple, of all sorts of shades and tones, in turban or robe—a perfect feast for the eye.

In the course of our drive through the bazaar we met no less than three wedding processions, though rather broken and interrupted by the traffic. In one the bridegroom (who, with the Hindus and Mohammedans, is considered the most important personage in the ceremony as well as the spectacle) was in a carriage, on his way to fetch the bride, in gorgeous raiment and with a crown upon his head. He was followed by people bearing floral trophies, perhaps intended for decoration afterwards. These consisted of gilt vases with artificial flowers in them, arranged in rows close together, and carried in convenient lengths on a plank or shelf by young men bearers.

Another of the bridegrooms was mounted on a horse, crowned and robed like a Byzantine emperor with glittering caparisons and housings, a tiny little dusky girl sitting behind him and holding on, who was said to be his little sister.

The third bridegroom we saw was veiled, in addition to the bravery of his glittering attire. Flowers were strewn by boys accompanying him, and a little bunch fell into our carriage as we waited for the procession to go by, in which, of course, the musicians went before. We afterwards passed the house where the wedding was being celebrated, the guests assembling in great numbers to the feast, a tremendous noise going on, drums beating and trumpets blowing. In one of the processions very antique-looking trumpets or horns were carried of a large size, much resembling the military horns of ancient Roman times. These were Hindu weddings.

We also had a glimpse of a Parsee wedding. This was in the open court of a large house arcaded from the street, brilliantly illuminated, where sat a great crowd of guests all attired in white.

Working right through the native bazaar we reached the Victoria Gardens, a sort of Kew and

Zoological rolled into one, being well stocked with fine palms and many varieties of tropical trees, as well as birds and animals, and all looking in good condition and well kept. Many Eurasians were here walking about, looking very weird in European dress. In these gardens are situated the Victoria and Albert Museum of Bombay.

Sir George Birdwood had given me an introduction to H.H. the Aga Khan and we drove out to his abode, only to find, however, that His Highness had gone to Calcutta on his way to Japan. I was not much more fortunate with my other introductions to the eminent Parsee Sir Jamsetji Jijibhai, and Sir Cowasji Jehangir Readymoney. Although the son of the latter magnate did call upon us and brought us an invitation from Lady Jehangir, we were unable to accept it owing to the shortness of our stay in Bombay. I understood that the Calcutta Races in December attracted a great many of the rich Bombay residents, and this accounted for the absence from their homes of many at that time.

We had a glimpse of some of the palaces on Malabar Hill, seeing the latter first against a glowing sunset. Fringed with palms and plantains, with its fantastic buildings silhouetted on the sky, it recalled the banks of storm cloud I had seen on the voyage, with their vaporous trees and aerial hanging gardens.

A closer acquaintance did not impress us with any conviction of the healthiness of Malabar Hill, though of the sumptuousness of its houses, and often their fantastic character, and the luxuriance of its palms and gardens, there could be no doubt. We passed the grey wall of the Tower of Silence, the burial (?) place of the Parsees, where the crows, the kites, and the vultures were gathered together, but did not linger there. From the hill there is certainly a magnificent view of the city of Bombay: especially if seen just before sundown, when a golden glow seems to transfigure the scene; and later, looking down on the vast plain, the white houses partly hid in trees scattered along the shore, the quays, and the ships at anchor in the bay, all seem to sink like a dream into the roseate atmosphere of sunset. But even that lovely light is darkened by a heavy smoke cloud drifting on the city from the forest of gaunt factory chimneys rising in the East like the shadow of poverty which is always cast by the riches of the West.

One rather wondered that Bombay was content to allow its best drive to be disfigured by a continuous succession of hideous commercial posters painted along the walls of one of its sides, the other being lined with palms and open towards the sea. This is, however, not worse indifference—in fact not so bad—as ours at home in allowing the posters along the railway lines to disfigure the charming and varied landscape of our own country.

One of the first necessities to the traveller in India, especially if he be ignorant of Hindustanee, is the engaging of a native bearer or servant. There is always a large class of these seeking engagements. They may be seen hanging about Messrs Cook's Tourist Offices in groups. They usually wear white clothes and turbans, but the half-caste Portuguese are dressed in semi-European fashion with their cloth suits and small, flat, round caps of

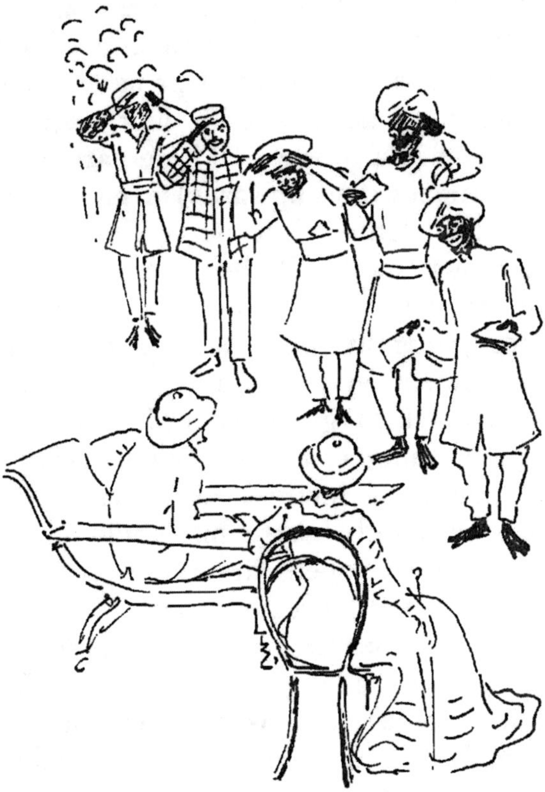

INTERVIEW WITH CANDIDATES FOR THE POST OF BEARER—MOSTLY UNBEARABLE!

the sort which used to be termed "pork pie" in England, only lower. These are embroidered round the rim, and a similar sort of head covering is also worn by superior caste Hindus. For the post of bearer the traveller will find plenty of applicants when he makes his requirements known, in fact their number is rather embarrassing, and they all produce "chits" or letters of recommendation from former employers. These, indeed, are the only references to go upon, unless one happens to come with the personal testimony of a friend. The bearers mostly register their names at Cook's offices, but they do not take any responsibility there for them in any way. These native servants expect 35 rupees (and upwards) a month, with an allowance for clothes, but out of this pay they find their own food. If, however, their food is provided, they take less pay—about 25 rupees—but prices generally have an upward tendency. The engagement may probably be for three or four months, which gives the ordinary European tourist time to get round India, visiting the principal places of interest *en route*. A rupee in India is now only worth one shilling and fourpence, and fifteen rupees are the equivalent of a sovereign, it should be remembered.

Of course the bearer's travelling expenses and washing are paid as long as he is with his master, and his fare home when his engagement comes to an end, and then, too, probably he would get a present if his conduct has been satisfactory. One does not generally expect mirrors of virtue and trustiness on such terms. No doubt native bearers vary considerably in capacity and experience as well as in appearance, to say nothing of honesty and fidelity, and some are better as couriers than as body or camp servants, or vice versa. Some claim to be efficient *valets des places* in addition to ordinary services, but it should be remembered that the bearer caste are not allowed to enter the sacred precincts of the great temples in India. Our choice, influenced mainly by a personal recommendation, fell on one Moonsawmy—a not unusual Hindu name. He had been in the service of Sir Samuel Baker and had had some experience in tiger-shooting, or at any rate had been out on such expeditions and in camp with the famous traveller and sportsman, but he had also acted as courier to English parties travelling in India, and professed to know the country well. We had planned an excursion to the caves of Ellora from Bombay with our friend M. Dauvergne, who had never seen them and was anxious to do so. Having mapped out our route we started on our expedition on December the 10th. Leaving Victoria Station, Bombay, at noon, we travelled by the G. I. P. (Great Indian Peninsular Railway), making our first train journey in India. The line crossed a cultivated plain at first, getting clear of Bombay ; groups of date palms here and there were suggestive of Egypt. We passed native villages of different types, some with thatched roofs and some with tile—brown ridge tiles not unlike what one sees in Italy, and even corrugated iron was visible (alas !) here and there. The low huts built of sun-dried bricks or mud with flat roofs were the strangest and most eastern-looking. One could get glimpses, too, of the inhabitants, the Hindu women in saris, often of red or purple or blue, bearing on their heads water jars or bright brass or copper vessels, with much natural grace, some also carrying little brown babies supported by one arm on their hip.

Leaving the plains we entered a very interesting hill country covered with jungle and forests where we saw many teak trees and banyans, besides many varieties of acacia. Mountains of striking form came into view, suggestive of castled crags. We soon afterwards passed the Thull Ghat, where the line rises as much as 1050 feet in a distance of about ten miles—which means a steep gradient. We passed rice fields, also sugar canes, and a kind of Indian corn, but not maize, and castor-oil plants which are cultivated extensively. There were interesting and picturesque groups of natives at all the stations. Finally Munmad was reached towards six o'clock in the evening. This was our first stage, and the junction for Daulatabad our next, in the territory of the Nizam of Hyderabad. We, however, decided to stay the night at Munmad and go on the next morning—in fact, if I remember right, it was a case of necessity, as there was no train on that evening. So we were conducted to the Dak Bungalow, some little walk from the station, through a native village, with our baggage carried on the heads of women coolies. We found the bungalow a most inhospitable place of incredible bareness, and nothing to sleep on but narrow wooden framed couches, having a sort of stringy webbing full of holes. The gaunt draughty rooms were almost destitute of other furniture and had no conveniences of any kind. The native keeper of the place seemed helpless. There was no food to be had, and he could not have cooked it if there had been, so we had to make shift as best we could with what we had in our tea baskets. I should not advise any one to travel in India, at least at all off the track of hotels, without provisions and bedding. There was not much sleep to be had that night. The beds were frightfully uncomfortable and the room was cold. An Anglo-Indian official on the forest service occupied the best room, we afterwards

A BED AT THE DAK BUNGALOW! MUMMAD (KEEP IT DA(R)K)

discovered, but he, as is usual, travelled with his horses and several servants, including a cook, and a supply of necessaries of all sorts. We left the inhospitable bungalow early the next morning, processing through the village in the same way as that in which we had come, with our baggage on the heads of the coolie women. We made the acquaintance at Munmad of the charming, frisky little palm squirrels which abound everywhere in India—delightful little greenish-grey creatures with dark longitudinal stripes extending from their noses to their tails. They play about the dwellings quite familiarly, but are off like a shot up a tree and out of sight at the smallest alarm. Scaling the trunk of a tree spirally, they have almost the appearance of lizards, and they are certainly as nimble.

The buffalo cow, too, is seen in every Indian village, a strange, dusky, rough-coated beast, with a weird, half-human, but rather sinister expression in its dark eyes, with long horns turned back upon their necks. They walk scornfully along to be milked, with an air which seems to say they thought the world but a poor place.

We took train to Daulatabad and entered the Nizam's territory. A police officer in his service was in the train, and was very intelligent and gave us much useful information. We now passed through a more arid-looking country than before, where cactuses and low trees grew sparsely on burnt yellow slopes and rocky hills, often of strange form, the country showing signs of a great upheaval from the sea.

At Daulatabad, a small road station, a tonga was waiting for us, drawn by two poor broken-down ponies and a rather ragged red-turbaned driver. Our destination was the town of Rozah, a drive of some ten miles and mostly uphill, on a loose, rough road.

A conspicuous object in the landscape at Daulatabad is the ancient fortress upon a steep hill rising abruptly from the plain. It was a famous stronghold, but was conquered by the Mohammedans in the thirteenth century. There are the ruins of the ancient city which it once protected, and within the citadel are remains of Hindu temples, one transformed into a mosque by the Moslems. Our road lay through the shattered gates which still marked the extent of the city with fragments of the outer walls, the whole area overgrown with trees and herbage, and clusters of native huts here and there. The road to Rozah is an almost continuous ascent, and in some places very steep, which made it very hard work for the wretched ponies which dragged our tonga, though, of course, we relieved it of our weight by walking up the worst hills. The sun was blazing, but there was a little shade to be had occasionally under the fine banyan trees which skirted the roadside.

Towards evening we saw the domes of Rozah on a high plateau in front of us, and presently entered the town through a battlemented gate. It was a Mohammedan town with many important domed tombs, but it had a neglected and sparsely peopled aspect and a look of departed splendour. We made our way along a straggling street, and, passing through another gate, came out upon the other end of the plateau, from which we saw, opening before us as far as the eye could reach towards the west, the vast, green, fruitful plains of the Deccan. In command of this view we found our quarters for the night—the Travellers' Bungalow—but this, the Nizam's bungalow, was a great contrast to the one at Munmad, being clean and comfortable, with good beds and sufficient furniture and rugs, and a bath-room. The native in charge was able to provide food, too, and to cook a dinner, which, if not exactly Parisian, was, at all events, a vast improvement upon our last one. The sun set without a cloud, the last golden light lingering upon the white and black domes of the tombs around us. Then followed the afterglow, and then the darkness fell like a curtain, but the stars were intensely bright in the clear sky. The air was very pure and the silence of the place was profound. We were glad to rest after our long, hot, dusty journey, but I managed to get a sketch done before the light went.

After breakfast the next morning (December 12) we started to walk to the caves at Ellora, which we found were only a short distance down the hill. A winding road led us past another of the Nizam's bungalows to a sort of terrace in front of the first great cave, or, more properly, rock-cut temple, the Kylas, which, coming down the hill from above, one does not see until close upon it, and it is only on entering the court through the great gateway that one slowly realises the wonder of it. A huge temple of symmetric ground plan cut clean out of the great cliff, the straight sides of which are seen rising like a vast wall above it. A mass of intricate and richly carved detail, a veritable incrustation of carving of extraordinary richness rises before one. Standing clear in a spacious court, enclosed on three sides by a deep arcade cut in the sheer sides of the cliff (which shows the tool marks), having an outer row of massive detached columns and an inner row of engaged columns, and deep recessed chambers.

On each side of the entrance to the temple in

THE KYLAS, CAVES OF ELLORA

the court stand two isolated columns or pylons, and near these two great stone elephants. These columns and elephants really flank a big pedestal

WE ARE INTRODUCED TO THE CAVES OF ELLORA

of stone with steps cut in it which lead up to a huge image of a Sacred Bull within a square chamber, from which a bridge is crossed and the portico of the temple is reached. Through this the great central hall, or nave, of the temple is entered, divided into four parts by groups of pillars, leaving an open passage up the middle and across to a portico on each side. From this chamber a few steps lead to the shrine of the Lingam, through a doorway. There are steps and doorways to each side of the shrine which lead on to open platforms, where are five recesses richly covered with sculptures of the Hindu mythology, as indeed is the whole temple, both within and without. The carved treatment and the whole idea of the scheme suggests that the original prototypes of such temples must have been structures of wood, and the elaborate treatment and small scale of some of the ornamental work seems reminiscent of wood-carving.

The carved work may be said to be of two kinds. There was a sort of architectural or formal ornament in low relief resembling in style and treatment Assyrian work, in which the lotus frequently appeared treated as a flat rosette and used as pateræ, arranged in rows with intervals; and there was a high relief treatment of figure sculpture. Among the horizontal courses of carved decoration I noted a treatment of the garland or swag, the ends being twisted through rings from which they were represented as depending. These might have been of a Greek or Roman pattern.

The exterior carving of the temple in the parts sheltered under eaves and by doorways showed traces of painting—the colours being red and green on white. The whole of the surfaces appear to have been coated with plaster to receive colour, in the same way as may be seen at the temple of Castor and Pollux at Girgenti.

The stone when exposed to the weather was very much blackened and resembled the gritstone of Derbyshire in colour and texture.

The Temple was dedicated to Siva, but the whole Hindu pantheon of the Vedic gods appeared to be sculptured in this marvellous place, as well as the different avators of Siva.

The Hindu religion is really a great system of nature-worship, all the powers, forces, and influences being personified and symbolised, nothing being accounted "common or unclean"—the elephant-headed Ganesha and the monkey god Hunuman taking their place as "eligible deities"—the whole scheme resting on the acknowledgment of the sexual origin of life. The generative organs themselves being revered as sacred, and symbolised in the mysterious Lingam which is enshrined in all the Hindu temples, and the object of special devotion.

The god Siva and Parvati his spouse form the principal subject among the sculptures of the Kylas. A striking design rather Egyptian in feeling was to be seen in a large carved panel of Parvati represented as seated on the water, or rather on a mass of lotus leaves and flowers—the flower of life—with attendant elephants symmetrically arranged on each side, showering water upon the goddess from their trunks. In all countries religious symbols are taken from familiar and characteristic objects common to each, although, as Count Goblet d'Albiella points out in his most interesting and learned work on the "Migration of Symbols," there is also a process of exchange and adaptation in ideas between different peoples and countries by means of which we get imported types, which, however, become naturalised and reappear in the form or convention peculiar to the country of their adoption.

As we gazed up at the cliffs from which this

AND ITS WASPS!

wonderful structure had been hewn, we noticed a number of green parrots fluttering about or clinging to the sheer walls of rock—like vivid green flashes of light upon the cold stone. Down in the court a number of extraordinarily large-sized wasps came buzzing about us. They looked formidable enough but did not do any damage, though their obtrusion did not facilitate the process of a sketching against time.

Besides the Kylas, which is said to date from about 750-850 A.D. There were a number of other and smaller temples, cut in the face of the cliff at intervals extending along the hill on each side of the Kylas. The most ancient is supposed to date from 200 B.C. and the latest from the thirteenth century A.D. A guide on the spot showed us several Buddhist temples and these were much more cave-like in character. One had very fine massive carved and fluted columns.

The second temple we saw suggested in its plan and form an apsidal basilica, and in detail wooden structure, the roof being carved in close ribs, curved to the form of a pointed arch, supported by a horizontal cornice and columns set very close together. A colossal figure of the seated Buddha filled the view at the end of the nave, but there was an ambulatory behind it. The figure was painted a dark red with white drapery and black hair, the eyes, with strongly marked white and black pupils, had a fixed stare which carried the whole length of the Temple.

The next temple visited, also Buddhistic, was much plainer, and was being supported by new buttresses of masonry to prevent the cliff from falling. The third was larger but also quite plain and square cut, the structure of the pillars and cornice being again on timber principles; but none approached the Kylas in beauty and interest.

The village of Ellora lay on the plain among trees about a mile and a half away from the foot of the cliff. Our guide pointed out some Jain temples there half hidden in masses of foliage and suggested a walk there, but by this time, between 10 and 11 o'clock in the morning, the sun was very powerful and the heat great, and as there was no shade till the village was reached and we had to get back to our bungalow, we gave it up and climbed the hill again. As we left the Kylas a large and most picturesque group of natives were squatted outside the gateway having a sort of picnic, a day out with their wives and numerous children, and they were wandering all over the temple chattering and laughing as they examined the sculptures and seemingly enjoying themselves much. They gazed at us curiously as we passed, as at some strange animals from an unknown country.

M. Dauvergne took some photographs of the caves, while I managed to get a coloured sketch of the Kylas, and a few notes.

We found the return journey to Daulatabad rather easier, being mostly downhill, though it was so precipitous in places that it was a marvel our poor ponies kept on their legs. We met many natives on the road, both Mohammedans and Hindus, as well as herds of goats, and asses with sacks of grain slung across their backs, black sheep and zebu carts.

We reached Daulatabad station about the middle of the day, or early afternoon, and were fortunate enough (owing to the language at the command of our friend who explained our wants) to get quite an excellently cooked and nicely served tiffin in the waiting-room.

There were interesting native figures about the station, and a group of figures at the village well not far off, where I got a sketch of a Hindu girl in a blue sari with a water jar on her head. She had a little round mark (Buddhist) like a red seal on her forehead, and her name was Hashuma.

We got a train about 5.30 back to Munmad arriving there soon after 9 at night. After dining at the station we bade farewell to our friend M. Dauvergne, who was travelling on to Bareilly, far up in the north-western provinces to join his shooting companion. Our train from Bombay did not leave until 3 A.M., but sleep was impossible owing to the noise, although we had a waiting-room to ourselves. It was only the usual conversazione which is carried on at every Indian station by the natives who throng the platforms, often waiting all night for a train, squatting in groups and keeping up a continual stream of talk. We were relieved when a faithful coolie announced the arrival of our train and carried in our bags. We had a compartment to ourselves for the most part until nearing Bombay, our only fellow-passengers being at different times a very quiet Hindu, and a British officer of the Royal Scots who did not travel far. But, before we got in, the carriage became crowded with every variety of costume, Parsee and Hindu merchants getting in for Bombay, until we were quite full up and—oh! so hot. Glad we were to get in at last, but not till noon—the hottest time of day — feeling rather fagged after our long journey. The heat in Bombay is very oppressive even in the so-called cool season. We generally lived in a temperature of about 88°, this in the dining-room being mitigated by electric fans; but it is always a relief when the sun declines, and a drive in the cool of the evening, is delightful.

We planned a rather extensive tour, and with the assistance of Messrs Cook, worked out a complete itinerary through India, ending at Ceylon, from whence we purposed to return in the following March.

On December 14 M. Dadabhai Naoroji arrived by the *Arcadia* at Bombay on his way to the National Congress at Calcutta of which he had been elected President. He had a great welcome. Flags and triumphal arches were put up along the esplanade, and he was brought from the Taj Mahal Hotel in a motor car decorated with flowers. An enormous crowd turned out to welcome him, chiefly of the Parsee community, and Parsees were conspicuous in the balconies of the houses and hotels along the route of the procession and parsee inscriptions of welcome hung across the streets. It was a striking scene from our balcony altogether. The last golden rays of the sun were slanting across the open esplanade alternating with broad luminous shadows and along the front streamed a vast white clad crowd—so different to the black crowds we are accustomed to in Europe—a white crowd varied with notes of bright colour and black here and there, and the red bunting floating around the

ARRIVAL OF MR. DADABHAI NAOROJI AT BOMBAY, DEC. 14, 1906

bronze equestrian statue of King Edward VII. in the foreground : while the balconies were gay with Parsee ladies in their delicate embroidered silks, canary coloured, pink, blue, green, violet and scarlet.

CHAPTER III

AHMEDABAD

WE left Bombay for Ahmedabad on December the 15th. Finding that the best train was a night one, and as it was a journey of some three hundred miles or more, and time was an object, we made up our minds, though not given to night travelling, to make an exception to our usual practice, although we should lose the sight of the country by the way. Railway travelling in India is quite as comfortable as one might expect. The carriages, it is true, vary on different lines and according to age, but, as a rule, the trains have separate carriages for Europeans and for different classes of natives, and it is often quite possible to have an entire compartment even for a long distance. On some lines the first-class carriages are scarcely better than the second, but the fare is double. The best carriages have compartments containing two long leather-covered seats, each side under the windows, which can be turned into sleeping couches at night. There is a good space between them and also at the end between the doors, and a lavatory is always attached. Above the seats are slung two upper berths, so that the compartment *could* be arranged for four sleepers. Any amount of light luggage can be taken into the compartments by passengers, but the heavy must be registered. The windows are protected from the sun by Venetian shutters, which can be let up or down, as well as glass, clear or toned, and sometimes fine wire screens. Outside there is a sort of hood, between which and the tops of the windows is a space for air, so that the fierce heat of the sun is tempered, and the carriage shielded to a certain extent from its rays.

We found very well-appointed sleeping-cars to Ahmedabad, but divided into ladies' and gentlemen's compartments. As it happened, another couple were the only others travelling by the first-class sleeping-car besides ourselves, so that we were able to arrange between ourselves that husbands and wives were not divided, each pair having a compartment to themselves.

Ahmedabad was reached about half-past seven in the morning. A crowd of coolies usually rush to seize your baggage on the arrival of a train, and our bearer was useful in keeping them at bay a bit. There was a Dak bungalow at Ahmedabad, but we did not feel any decided leaning towards it, and, finding there were quite decent bedrooms to be had at the station and that we could feed in the refreshment-room, we decided to stay there.

Carriages were to be had at from six to eight rupees a day, and we engaged one and had a drive through the town, stopping to see the mosques for which it is so famed. The Jama Musjid had a splendid, spacious court in front of it, walled around, the entrance being through a rather small door, where it is necessary for the visitors either to put off their shoes or to consent to have enormous loose ones of grass or matting tied on over their own, which seems to prevent desecration quite as efficiently. The mosque had fifteen domes, and

THE FEET OF PILGRIMS (AT MOHAMMEDAN MOSQUES)

inside was a forest of white pillars (260), and a large gallery for the women, screened with pierced stone-work in lovely patterns. There were the marble tombs of Ahmad Shah—the builder of the mosque—and his son and grandson, richly carved in delicate relief, the sides being arcaded, and under each arch the representation of a hanging lamp, or censer, some of the latter showing an ornamental treatment of smoke ascending from them.

The marble pavements had a peculiar fine dull polish, noticeable in mosque pavements throughout India, which is the result of the constant movement of the bare feet of the natives passing over their surface. The tombs of the queens of Ahmad Shah were carved with remarkable fineness. One, inlaid with delicate trees in white marble or black, was as fine as any Persian cabinet work in ivory.

The Queen's Mosque, with three domes, contains charming carving and pierced screen-work.

The mosque of Rani Sipri and her tomb are marvellously rich in fine carving in red sandstone and screen-work, and suggest in some of their forms and the rich incrustation of their ornament the influence of Hindu work, which, indeed, is a characteristic of many here. Beautiful pierced screens of stone-work, divided into panels by the supporting columns, enclose the tomb.

For the loveliest designs, however, in pierced screen-work, one still turns to those of the windows of the Sidi Sayyids' Mosque, especially to the two wherein palms and rose-trees are combined in a sort of natural formation to form a lovely mesh of intricate, yet perfectly coherent and balanced pattern, which fills the tympanum shape of low-arched windows; a design in light on dark seen from the outside, and in dark against light seen from within, when it fulfils its purpose of breaking up the light of the sun, and producing that enchanting luminous twilight so characteristic of Eastern interiors. There are reproductions of two of these windows at our Indian Museum at South Kensington, but I had long desired to see the originals, and I was not disappointed. The warm light of the

POOR RELATIONS

late afternoon sun lingered in their interstices, and, seen from below, the under sides of the marble fret took rich golden reflections, which gave the designs quite a new aspect, and filled them with life and colour, giving the effect almost of sunlit foliage. We drove to see Shah Alam's Mosque, built about 1420, which was reached in about half an hour beyond the city gates, along a cool avenue of acacias. The mosque has a fine court and minarets, and a splendid canopied tomb, with pillars inlaid with mother-o'-pearl; beautiful metal-work in pierced brass gates and screens.

On returning from this drive we stopped near the river Sarbarmati in a grove of trees, chiefly banyan, mango, and acacia. Here a native boy set up a peculiar hooting sort of call, and presently we saw troops of silver-grey monkeys dropping from the trees and gambolling along towards us between the stems—hundreds of them apparently —hurrying up to feed on the dried peas we scattered for them. They came crowding around us, but were quite friendly, and many would feed out of our hands. They varied much in size, but were mostly large, and carried their tails high in the air and curled over their backs in spirited curves when walking on all-fours. Many of the female monkeys carried their young ones with them. All looked beautifully clean and healthy, and were full of play —in fact as different as possible in their freedom from the poor captives in cages at zoological gardens. It was amusing to watch their pranks and to note the ease with which they would climb up into the trees, some of which were as full of monkeys almost as branches.

As we left the monkeys we had another unusual sight. We saw a large and leafy mango tree leaning over the river, which seemed to have suddenly burst into white blossoms; but we soon perceived these supposed flowers begin to flutter, and winged ones detached themselves from the mass of white, which we then discovered were white cranes. They would rise in a cloud and settle again ever and anon among the green foliage. They were a small kind,

A FAMILY PARTY—CRANES ON A MANGO TREE (SARBARMATI RIVER)

not larger than a heron, and are common all over India. We often saw them afterwards rising by the side of the pools by the railway track, or fishing, or flying over the submerged paddy fields, but in smaller numbers, and never so beautifully.

On the white and dusty road to Ahmedabad we met numbers of wagons loaded with cotton bales and drawn by large white oxen. The country carts had wicker bodies, somewhat like those I have seen in Germany, and primitive massive wheels with eight spokes in a double cross. Camels were occasionally seen ridden by natives. As at Bombay, there were extensive cotton factories here, and cotton was very largely grown in the country around.

The bazaars and the street life in Ahmedabad are most various and interesting, all sorts of trades and crafts being carried on. There is still a great quantity of silk-weaving done, and brocades wrought with gold thread. A proverb of the place quoted by Mr W. S. Caine has it that the prosperity of Ahmedabad hangs on three threads—"gold, silk, and cotton"; and these three threads still symbolise the main industries of the city. A picturesque incident in the streets is the silk-winder—in some open space in front of the shops you may sometimes see a native woman standing (like Mr Holman Hunt's "Lady of Shalott") within a low square enclosure formed of bamboo sticks wound with long strands of silk thread. She holds a sort of spindle in her left hand, and a long tapering wand in her right, by means of which she divides or regulates the thread as she winds it off on to the bamboo sticks, rapidly twirling the spindle as she does so. It is an extremely pretty and picturesque sight. The old methods of hand-weaving are practised, and for weaving the brocades or "kincobs" the treadles in the loom are lifted from above by a boy, who draws up the cords attached to the threads of the warp according to the pattern the weaver is working. It is said that the native trade in the finer brocaded silks has been injured owing to the richer natives following the European fashion of dressing plainly, the rich silk woven with gold thread being only worn on state occasions, another instance of the depressing influence of Western ideas and habits upon the East. The rich merchants, and the Maharajahs and their court officials no doubt believe they are improving their style in adopting fashions from Europe, but the effect is practically only to vulgarise the native taste. The native princes and the well-to-do merchants now dash about in imported motor cars in raiment of dingy tints, instead of proudly prancing upon stately elephants and clothed in splendour and colour. Eastern life is made less joyous in its aspects by such changes. The mass of the people do not change, however, and seem to have no desire to, and they are the common people everywhere who give the characteristic life and colour. Though they only wear cotton or muslin, the beauty and variety of the tints are wonderful, and fill the bazaars with a stream of ever-changing hues in the most unexpected combinations and harmonies.

Driving through the bazaars at Ahmedabad, we came to a sort of open space from which several streets diverged, and here was being held a sort of open market of cloth—chiefly muslins and cottons of every variety of colour and pattern. These were laid out in piles on the ground, the merchants squatting by their goods or spreading them out to show their customers.

We stopped our carriage, and got our bearer to bring us some of the stuffs to look at and to inquire the prices, and we were soon surrounded by an

STREET SCENE, AHMEDABAD
ENGLISH TRAVELLERS SKETCHING AND MAKING PURCHASES

eager crowd of dark faces and turbaned heads, and were nearly buried in a rainbow-tinted cloud of muslin and cotton cloth, amid which deliberate selection became difficult. I noted, however, many examples of the native method of dyeing cloths in patterns by the tying and dipping methods which often produce most delightful results, the pattern having a softer and more blended effect than the ordinary block printing. Although Manchester cottons were in evidence, it was pleasant to see that native methods were not forgotten, and were still in demand.

The native pottery, too, at Ahmedabad is extremely interesting, the common forms are always good, as indeed they are throughout India. Enormous earthen jars are made here to hold grain, or for carrying water from the river on ox-carts. The ordinary earthen water-jar, which the Hindu women carry on their heads, resembles the ancient Greek Hydria in form, and is so beautiful that it is distressing to see it occasionally substituted by the hideous tin kerosine can—another European innovation—much more difficult to balance one would think. In the streets of Ahmedabad occasional features are small, richly-carved octagonal minarets supported on posts, and looking like glorified pigeon houses. There is a big Hindu temple—a Jain temple of no antiquity, only about thirty or forty years old. The shrine of Hathi Sing. It has the characteristic pagoda domes, and is elaborately painted and decorated, though rather coarsely. The finest features were the marble pavements where, again, one noticed the peculiar soft polish given by bare feet.

A very interesting excursion is that to Sarkhei, a drive of about seven miles outside the city gates. The road crosses the wide river Sarbarmati—or rather its bed, as the water shrinks into a rather narrow stream, and is almost lost sometimes among great stretches and banks of sand. At the water's edge, as we passed, we saw the people busy washing clothes (which made a pretty coloured pattern

TOMB OF GUNJ BAKSH, SARKHEI

when spread on the sands to dry) or themselves, or watering horses and bullocks, or refreshing their baskets of vegetables they had borne along the dusty ways by dipping them in the stream.

Our road was deep in dust, but generally pleasantly shaded by fine old trees, chiefly banyan, teak trees, and acacias. The little striped squirrels were very numerous and active, frisking up and down and around the tree stems. Monkeys were occasionally seen—of the same silver grey sort we had seen on our visit to the Mosque of Shah Alam—in the jungles at the side of the road, or in the trees. A bird rather like a large bullfinch was common, and we saw many peacocks wandering about, and, of course, kites and crows everywhere. On the road we passed many a heavy-laden ox-cart, piled with bales of cotton, making their way to Ahmedabad, as well as droves of white asses, and many groups of natives. About two miles out we saw at the side of the road a large brick-built Mohammedan Tomb, said to be the tomb of the architect of Sarkhei, who was a Persian.

Further on our carriage turned out of the main road down a narrow lane to the right and up a steep bit of hill, flagged with flat stones. Presently we arrived in front of a fine gateway of Moslem architecture, which formed the entrance to a large quadrangle, shaded by a very old acacia tree. We had to put on the usual clumsy canvas shoes before entering this court, which enclosed the splendid mosque and tomb of Gunj Baksh (begun by Mahmudshah in 1445 and finished by Begara in 1451), with a low, flat cupola, and many pilastered front, the structures of the caps showing Hindu influence. There is a finely worked lattice screen of brass surrounding the octagonal shrine within, containing the tomb. The floor is inlaid with coloured marbles, and the roof is rich with gilding. An open pavilion stood in the court in front of the shrine, raised upon a platform, with steps supported by sixteen carved marble pillars. Opposite to this is a charming portico, through which one can get a glimpse of the great tank, though it was almost dried up when we saw it, the water hardly enough to conceal an alligator, though white cranes were standing in the pool in the forlorn hope of catching fish, and monkeys gambolled about the steps. On the side of the court near the entrance are the tombs of Mahmud Begara and his two sons—of the usual Mohammedan type, an arcaded pattern in low relief along the sides; with censers hanging between the arches of similar type to those at Ahmedabad.

There is a pathetic feeling of departed or half decayed splendour about Sarkhei, as well as a sense of romance and mystery, and one leaves it impressed with the idea of the refinement, sense of beauty, and spaciousness of the departed princely builders who lie buried within their own architectural dream.

There are always a number of hangers on about Indian tombs and temples, self-constituted guides, and persons of indefinite status and occupation who cluster around the arriving and departing stranger, who has to smooth his path with backsheesh, and Sarkhei is no exception. We had a hot drive along the dusky highway back to Ahmedabad in the middle of the day, the sun blazing down very fiercely, and we were glad of the protection of the carriage hood.

In the course of one of our evening drives about the town, our Moonsawmy pointed out an acacia tree we passed by the roadside which appeared to be full of what looked like large pendant pear-shaped fruit of black and golden brown colour. These, however, were really clusters of fruit-bats hanging in the tree until nightfall. Some of them, as we looked, were already moving and stretching out their wings in the last rays of the evening sun.

We passed through the triple arched ancient gateway which stands at the head of the main street. The bazaars were crowded with buyers and sellers, chiefly of cotton and other stuffs. The people themselves in every variety of costume formed a wonderful scheme of colour, varied by the brownskins of babies and little children playing about quite naked, and the brown backs of the workers bending over their crafts. The whole scene fused in the light of after-glow and rich in tone and chiaroscuro.

CHAPTER IV

AHMEDABAD TO AJMIR

THE railway station at Ahmedabad has the unusual distinction of two striking minarets of brick-work, richly cut and moulded in successive circular tiers, which rise to a considerable height from amid the palms and plantains of a small well-watered Eastern garden, with many straight-cut paths between the thickly planted trees. These are the remains of a Mohammedan mosque which once stood there. It is an unusually interesting and pleasant place to wander in while waiting for a train.

Our bearer secured a comfortable coupé for our journey to Ajmir, which was to be our next halting-place. We had originally intended to visit Mount Abu to see the wonderful Jaiṇ temples of Delwara, but before we reached the Abu road heavy rain came on, and as it would have meant a pony ride of sixteen miles from the station to Mount Abu, we decided to go on to Ajmir without a break.

Leaving Ahmedabad at 8.15 we breakfasted in the train, there being a restaurant car put on. The trains not being corridor trains it is necessary to get out at the stopping stations and find one's way to the car and back to one's carriage again.

The country at first was very flat and generally

cultivated, but with occasional belts of jungle, where monkeys and peacocks were seen. Fine banyan and acacia trees here and there. Ploughing with oxen was going on, and the yoke of oxen drawing at the irrigation wells was a frequent sight.

About the middle of the day dark clouds rolled up and we had a heavy shower with promise of more to come. Mountains came into view at the same time as the change in the weather, and it was not long before we reached Abu Road Station. The fine mountain range on the left of the line amid which Mount Abu was situated was veiled in cloud and rain, but as we left the mountains the sky cleared again, and we entered a flat, desert-like region covered with stunted trees or dry scrub bush, stretching for miles. A strange-looking country was afterwards traversed, where huge granite boulders lay on the earth like mounds and partly overgrown, others might have been imagined to be the shells of gigantic tortoises. At a station called Mori this characteristic was the most striking. The stations on this line through Rajpootana were built after the Moslem fashion and had a superficial resemblance to mosques, being domed, the smaller buildings and wayside signal huts being treated in the same manner.

After a rainy sunset of orange and grey, darkness soon fell, and it was not long before we reached Ajmir after about twelve hours' travel—a distance of over three hundred miles. We found fairly comfortable quarters at the station refreshment-rooms, the bedrooms being above and opening on to spacious terraces from which interesting views of the town and country could be had. The only drawbacks were the noises. What with the shrieks of the engines, and the perpetual conversazione carried on on the platforms, which were generally thronged with most picturesque crowds of natives, sleep was very broken.

Ajmir is very beautifully situated, with a fine background of hills, the town itself being on a slope with an old fort crowning a height immediately above it. There is a large military station, the cantonments with the residency and the English bungalows lying on a plain quite away from the native town.

We hired a carriage and drove around the town the morning after our arrival, visiting the old palace and massive fortress built by the Emperor Akbar, who has left so many noble buildings in the north-west of India to testify to his power and influence in the past. We entered through a noble gateway into a large quadrangle surrounded by tremendously high, thick walls and having octagonal bastions at four corners. A pavilion rose in the centre of the court, raised upon a platform led up to by steps of marble. Extensive restorations were being carried on under the Indian Government, so much so that one had fears they were in danger of going too far in the direction of renewal, and did not draw the line with sufficient decision at the limits of preservation and repair. Certainly new work was being put in freely. It was interesting, however, to see that most beautiful and characteristic Indian craft of piercing patterns in marble being carried on. The native carver, turbaned and grey-bearded, was squatting on the ground busy with a small marble grill or screen. He was drilling a geometric diaper pattern through a panel of marble which had a worked moulding for frame. The slab was bedded in clay to keep it from under the worker's hands, and to prevent splitting. When the holes were drilled he finished the work with chisels and mallet, working out the different bevels and facets of the quatre-foils, and putting in the work that which gave all the richness and the effect of the pattern. He seemed pleased to have his work noticed, and anxious that we should see it in its finished state he went to where a group of native women were at work on other similar grills which had left the carver's hands, cleaning the pierced patterns from the clay, and showed the completed panels clear cut in the white marble. It was noticeable that the women only did the cleaning and polishing up, but not the carving.

We had a fine view from the ramparts and minarets of the pavilion.

From the fort we went on driving through the bazaars of Ajmir, which were highly interesting but less busy and crowded, perhaps, than at Ahmedabad. Gay coloured cottons and muslins, embroidered slippers, pottery, and grain of all kinds were mostly in evidence, the latter arranged in heaps on cloths spread on the ground in front of the shops, and measured out by the traders squatting by their merchandise. The fronts of the native houses here were mostly in white plaster, often painted with designs in blue and yellow of formal flowers in vases, or quaint animals and figures in profile.

There was much fancy and variety in the design of the little arcaded projecting balconies corbelled out from the wall, and ogee arched windows, and moulded plaster and painted ornament.

We presently, at the end of the principal street, approached the magnificent double gateway of the famous Dargah—named the Dilkasha (or "heart-expanding") gate. From the street one really sees three ogee arches of different heights in succession, one beyond the other, the highest being flanked by towering minarets crowned with cupolas. The whole gateway in the bright morning sunlight looked a fairy-like aerial structure, fair and white, and glittering here and there with gold, and tile patterns in blue and yellow.

The Dargah of Ajmir is revered as the burial-place of one Kwaja Sahib, a saint of the thirteenth century. His beautiful white and gold domed shrine enclosing his silver tomb occupies the centre of the inner court, and is visited by troops of pilgrims. A great festival is held in honour of the saint every year, when Ajmir is thronged with pilgrims. Two enormous iron pots are shown, standing each side the entrance to the Dargah, in which at the festival are cooked tons of food freely given to the pilgrims. The biggest pot is reputed to hold no less than 10,000 lbs. of food. The food consists of mess of rice, oil, sugar, raisins, and almonds, which is rather suggestive of a sort of plum pudding, and on this scale costs about £100.

On first entering the Dargah through the great gateway one sees a large paved court with several domed tombs and a mosque, and rising high the

SHRINE OF THE KWAJA, AJMIR

old fort of Tarrgarh, white-walled on the brown hill, is seen above. I noted a very fine bronze many-branched candelabra on one of the domed tombs. Passing through this court the second court is entered where stands the shrine. It is surrounded by a low marble balustrade, and is picturesquely overshadowed by a large ancient ilex tree, through the spreading branches of which with their masses of rich dark foliage glows the colour and gold of the richly decorated shrine. Through the open doors gleam the silver of the tomb, and the ivory-like dome fretted and crested with gold sparkling in the full light of the sun pierces the deep blue sky. Curious low tapering pedestals with small cupolas at the top are placed about the courts and around the shrine at intervals. These are pierced with small recesses, in which, on festival occasions, small lamps are placed. Beyond the shrine we come out upon a high-walled terrace which extends with a succession of bays along the sides of a deep narrow tank, flights of steps leading down to the water's edge at different points.

It is the custom when visitors leave the Dargah for the attendants to hang garlands of flowers about their necks, and in return for this graceful attention an offering to the shrine—or to its hangers on—is expected.

The visitor is, however, rather carefully watched inside the Dargah. The shrine itself is not allowed to be entered. Shoes must be removed on entering the court, or the big canvas shoes put on over them. On sketching intent I was not allowed to pitch a camp stool near the shrine or in the sacred precincts, and even open umbrellas, for shade, were objected to by these jealous watchful devotees.

From the Dargah we went to see the roofless mosque of "Arhai-din-ka-Jhonpra," which being interpreted signifies "The house of two and a half days." It is on the hill opposite the fort, but on the lower slope, and is approached through narrow streets, and finally reached by a steep flight of steps which lead to the gateway of the court of the mosque. It is now little more than a beautiful red sand-stone carved screen of open pointed arches, but the detail is exceedingly rich and happy in scale, and largely consists of bordering inscriptions outlining the arches and their rectangular framings, the texts being in both Cufic and Togra characters, and both these and the surface decoration generally are delicately but sharply cut in sunk carving, which preserves a certain unity of ornamental effect. Arranged along the side of the court are many carved fragments which are the remains of the Jain Temple, transformed into the Mussulman Mosque in the year 1236 by Altamash, who conquered the city, and was said to have effected the transformation in two and a half days.

The mosque was not used for worship. In the court a rope or cord maker was at work. The white strands stretched over canes from the man working at one end of the walk to where at the other end his assistant sat at a sort of wheel by means of which the strands were twisted into a cord of the required thickness.

After this we drove to the Daulat Bagh (Garden of splendour)—then passing through a beautiful park full of pine-trees we came to the white marble pavilion built by Shah Jehan, standing on a marble balustraded terrace, and overlooking a lovely lake, bounded by mountains—a lovely spot. The pavilion has been restored by the Indian government, and looks quite new. Marble, however, does not seem to weather or discolour in the Indian climate, and the difference between new and old is not nearly so marked as in European countries, while the imitative faculty of the Hindu workman and the traditions of craftsmanship under which he still works help to complete the illusion when restoration is done. New or old, it was an enchanting place, especially when the evening sun floods the whole scene with golden light, streaming through the trees, and filling the marble porticoes with warm colour. The lake still as a mirror, reflecting the fairy palace and the dreamy distance in its glassy surface. The chief commissioner should be happy to have his residence in the midst of this lovely garden. The lake is as useful too as it is beautiful, as from it is obtained the water supply of Ajmir.

Another of our evening drives was through the cantonments outside the native city. We passed through the English military quarters, and saw the long low barrack-like bungalows of the soldiers, clean and neat, but bare and ugly. There were more comfortable bungalows of the officers and other English residents in gardens and amid trees, with entrance gates and drives, almost suburban, allowing for little differences in detail. The names of the residents, for instance, were painted in white block letters on ugly black boards placed outside the gates of the gardens. There was the usual club-house in a landscape garden, and here a military band of native infantry was playing, conducted by a man in a straw hat. English ladies, and children with their native aejahs and bearers scattered about the lawns.

On the road a little distance from the town a large number of natives were busy making up the road over a new bridge across the railway. Many of these coolies were very attenuated, and might have come from the famine districts.

Passing through the bazaar on my return from sketching in the Dargah, I noticed among the stalls of a crowded and picturesque native street a craftsman at work putting a border pattern upon the edge of a piece of orange-coloured muslin. He first printed or stamped the border, a small leaf and flower pattern, from a wood block with some sort of size of a brown colour, and when this was sufficiently "tacky" he laid on silver leaf over the pattern thus defined by the block in size, and finished by brushing away the superfluous leaf with a soft brush, much as our gilders do.

A quaint effect was produced by the camels here, laden with great sheafs of sugar-cane, which trailed behind, spreading out over their hind quarters in a way that suggested skirts or a crinoline—viewed from behind.

From our terrace over the railway station we could observe the varied groups of natives which continually thronged the platforms and the yards outside. Certainly the native in India makes constant use of the railways, although the railways do not take any trouble to make them comfortable. The native carriages seem always in an overcrowded state, and many of them are rather

THE CAMEL'S CRINOLINE (SUGAR CANE) AJMIR

suggestive of cattle trucks with rough wooden partitions. Troups of natives will come to a railway station and camp all night waiting for some train in the morning. On inquiring what classes or manner of people these poor travellers mostly were, I was told that they comprised chiefly pilgrims to various shrines and festivals in different parts of the country, and small traders. The Ryot, or agriculturist, did not travel much, as might be supposed. The people usually bore great bundles with them, bedding presumably, and other necessaries for long journeys. These the women carried upon their heads. In the evenings groups of natives would be seen gathered round fires made on the ground. These were often mere flares of straw, and did not last very long, though they may have served to mitigate the chill of the nightfall, which is always so sudden in India.

As evidence of the extraordinary variety of colour arrangements in the costume of the natives in the bazaars, here are a few notes made of the colours worn by passers-by, both men and women, at Ajmir observed in the course of a few minutes.

1. Citron tunic, emerald green turban, white trousers.

2. Buff turban black tunic, white trousers.

3. (Woman.) Large vermilion cloak, pink skirt.

4. Pea green turban, crimson velvet tunic, white trousers.

5. Orange turban, black tunic, white trousers.

6. White turban, wound round a red fez, deep brown orange cloak thrown over brown jacket and white breeches.

7. Orange muslin simply covering head and body, scarlet trousers. (Mohammedan woman.)

8. Turquoise turban, golden orange tunic (long) lined with pale yellow.

The agricultural country folks generally wore white, though it was rather a dusky white. Groups of herdsmen were occasionally seen with long straight wands, their dark faces and bare limbs emerging from white cotton turbans, tunics and cloaks.

Travellers in India as well as English residents are often greeted with salaams in the native bazaars and passers-by on the road. The word "salaam" is pronounced by natives sometimes in a tone almost of command, but as far as I could understand it was intended to suggest a mutual exchange of salutations, or even the word alone might be taken as a salutation sometimes; but it is always expected that an answering salute of some kind will be given, but it is said that one should never salute with the left hand if it is wished to avoid offence. The ordinary mode of salutation in any country should be carefully observed, as in no way can offence be more easily given, however inadvertently, by any apparent neglect of what are considered the ordinary courtesies of life sanctioned by the customs of a country.

It is true that the native children seemed sometimes inclined to mock at a stranger, in a spirit of monkey mischief, perhaps, but there are little street gamins in any city, and the latest product of our civilisation, the London street arab, would be difficult to beat anywhere, East or West.

CHAPTER V

CHITORGARH AND UDAIPUR

FROM Ajmir there is a branch line to Chitorgarh and Udaipur, and no traveller in India should miss the opportunity of visiting both these highly interesting places. Leaving Ajmir, the railway runs south through a rather flat country, passing Naisirabad, an important British military station. The English "Tommy" in khaki, and white helmet and putties, or the sun-burned, brown-booted and spurred British cavalry officer, were in evidence at the railway station. Among the native crowd here we saw a turbaned man in pink carrying a very thin, aged woman, probably his mother, pick-a-back fashion.

A very dry and almost desert tract of country is traversed after this, though occasionally varied by irrigated fields and green crops. The irrigation wells, worked by oxen as before, and the native ploughing, were the chief incidents in the landscape. The plough is a very primitive-looking implement with a single shaft, with a cross handle fixed at right angles to the shaft, which consists of a sharpened piece of wood, tipped with iron. The plough is drawn by a pair of zebus, and is light enough for the man to lift up and turn at the end of the furrow, or even to be carried home on his shoulder at the end of the day. There were thick hedges of spikey sort of cactus, branching out from a main stem, something like candelabra, the fronds growing in a longitudinal, rigid form. These hedges fenced the railway line from the fields on the desert. Another plant of common occurrence, both here and all over India, was a broad-leaved shrub of symmetric order, having small, pale, lilac flowers, the stems rather a yellow, and the leaves a lightish blue green. We noted also a sort of wild laburnam. The prickly pear was common, and a sort of prickly acacia-like shrub much liked by camels. The trees were mostly various acacias, the banyan tree (Ficus), and the teak. In places we saw both date and cocoa palms. At one station (Mandal) the level plains, with pyramidal hills in the distance and a grove of palms and camels in the foreground, again recalled Egypt.

The cultivated crops we passed were cotton, tobacco, rice, wheat, and sugar cane.

At every station may be seen the water filter, a wooden tripod stand, holding three red earthen water-jars, one above the other. The natives drink quantities of water, and always carry a small drinking-vessel of bright brass, which they take every opportunity of filling. The water-bearer is a characteristic figure everywhere, and comes up to the train with his cry, "Panee! panee!" which (with an Italian prepossessed ear) is more suggestive of another, and solid, necessary of life. Bread, however, in Hindustanee, happens to be "roti."

Having left Ajmir by the 9.20 A.M. train, we arrived at Chitorgárh about five in the evening, and put up at the station rooms for the night. There was a considerable crowd on the long, open, gravelled platform, mainly natives, with a small contingent of English and American tourists. European tourists in India, however, were generally few and far between, the United States being much more numerously represented. A picturesque group was formed by a native resident from Udaipur, with his retinue, waiting for their train on. The chief was a venerable and a kindly-looking man, with white hair and beard, reminding one rather of the late G. F. Watts. He was gaily dressed in a pink turban and a lilac silk coat, and was seated on a chair on the platform, surrounded by his attendants in scarlet; among these was his trumpeter, with a bugle slung around him, and a quad of four soldiers in khaki and turbans.

We found the Traveller's Bungalow was about three-quarters of a mile or so away from the station. The bedrooms were all taken by the English and American parties, but we could feed there, so, retaining our quarters at the station, we walked to the Bungalow for our dinner. It was a lovely moonlight night, with bright stars, but there was a cold north wind as we were guided by our bearer with a lantern along a rather rough track, and crossed the railway to the Bungalow, a new stone building, bare and cheerless as they make them, standing all by itself in a stoney yard without a tree near it. The dinner, or supper, was not very rewarding, and we trudged back again to the station in the cold moonlight. The station we found quieter than usual. The servants of the resident had encamped upon the platform, and formed picturesque groups around fires, cooking and gossiping; their master sleeping in the train, which was drawn up ready to start for Udaipur early the next morning.

It seems highly necessary for travellers in India anywhere off the track of hotels to provide themselves with bedding of some sort, at least quilts, rugs, sheets, and pillows. The nights at this time of year in Rajpootana are quite cold, and warm wraps are welcome.

The next morning we engaged a large elephant —which waited at the station to take travellers to Chitorgarh—to carry us to the fort and deserted city on the height we could see from the station. This was a distance of some seven miles there and back, it was said.

The elephant was made by the driver to kneel while we mounted, by means of a ladder of bamboo, and seated ourselves on the flat, cushioned seat, having a low hand-rail and a foot board, slung by ropes. The elephant moved with a peculiar swaying, swinging movement, not unlike that of a ship, though regular. We started over a stretch of rough, common-like ground, broken into hillocks and hollows, overgrown with scrub bush, the track not being very definite. The elephant picked its way most carefully over the rough parts, especially when descending a hollow. We reached a roadway which led over a bridge across a river, and brought us up to the city of Chitor at the foot of the hill, and extending upon its lower slopes. We entered the city through a Moslem arched gateway, and threaded our way through the narrow streets, our elephant filling the whole of the road-way. Pottery, beads, glass bracelets, cheap lacquered

FIRST ELEPHANT RIDE. (CHITORGARH)

ornaments, and small merchandise of various kinds were spread out on the ground, their proprietors squatting by their stock in trade. The native houses were small and low, for the most part hardly more than huts of mud, roofed with sun-baked tiles, laid scalewise over a trellis of bamboo, often very dilapidated. There were remains of better houses and older, with arcaded balconies, and here and there we passed a small white-washed temple, with quaint elephants with gay housings painted in profile on the white walls each side the entrance. These elephants are drawn in a very spirited manner, and are generally represented going at a trot, and full of action with trunk and tail in the air, decorated with bells on his feet and gorgeous red and yellow housings and domed howdah, set off by the solid black of the elephant and his ivory tusks, the turbaned driver flourishing his goad. From our commanding eminence, the elephant's back, we could take a comprehensive survey of the life of the city, and see the people at work at various trades. The inhabitants did not take much notice of us; some would stare and others would salaam as we passed. I imagine the elephant with European travellers on its back not infrequently passed through Chitor, although we managed to startle a tethered camel in one of the streets considerably, and the animal tugged at its rope and plunged alarmingly at the sight of our elephant.

Leaving the city of Chitor, which seemed very poverty-stricken, we reached the first gate of the fortress, and began the ascent of some 200 or 300 feet. The road zig-zags up the side of the rocky plateau, upon the summit of which the fort and ancient city were built, the ancient capital of Rajpootana. Massive walls protect this road on the outer side, and a continuous warder's walk runs along it, with flights of stone steps to the roadway at intervals. We passed through five gateways on the way up, generally enriched with sculptured ornament—the last one, Ram Pol, being the richest, and this was finely carved with Hindu detail and symbols, having friezes of elephants. There have been extensive restorations at Chitorgarh. The whole length of the wall seems to have been gone over, and replastered, and in many places rebuilt with new stone. The tops of the gates were crenellated in a fashion which suggested a perpetuation in stone of an earlier type of wooden palisading, a horizontal band connecting the rounded or pointed stone heads, the divisions between each being continued below it. In many cases the old massive wooden gates were left under the archways, bound with old iron bands. By the way, at Ajmir we noted that the wooden doors of the gateways to the courts were covered with old horse-shoes nailed on, close together, in some instances actually over the old rich carved work, and apparently with the same idea of good omen as is associated with the same emblem in our country.

Arrived at the summit there were wonderful ruins to be seen. Scattered over the plateau, half overgrown, amid heaps of shattered stones and carved fragments, there were the remains of Mohammedan palaces and Hindu or Jain Temples, rich within and without with intricate carving.

The guides showed us where the Hindu Queen and the women of the city, all suffocated themselves in a subterranean chamber to escape their fate had they fallen into the hands of the Mohammedan conquerors, when Ala-ud-din took Chitor by storm in 1290.

The hand of the restorer was seen here again

and had been in some parts rather too thorough. I noticed an arcade over the gateway of the Moslem Palace, which seemed to have been entirely rebuilt in a kind of pale green marble, almost the colour of jade, quite sharply cut and new, and out of keeping with the old work more or less battered and ruined around it. The famous Tower of Victory had been extensively restored, even the carving in parts recut. This is going too far, as it is impossible to unite modern workmanship with old, even in India. Watchful and careful, timely repair is the only way to preserve ancient buildings, but there should be no attempt made to replace lost carving and decoration by modern imitation.

We entered over broken steps a wonderful Jain temple, very richly carved, with a remarkable domed ceiling over the central chamber, arranged in a series of concentric circles, intersected by figures of dancing girls, with emblems radiating from the centre. Another Jain temple formed a most picturesque pile, and a delightful mass of light and shade filled in with intricate detail, in the full sunlight. In these temples a favourite deity is Ganesha, the elephant-headed god, whose carved image constantly appears.

In one part of the ancient city we came upon some natives preparing cotton yarn for hand weaving. The yarn was stretched in long lengths across horizontal canes supported by vertical ones. They seemed to be cleaning the threads with combs and brushes. The little black-bristled hand-brushes placed on the top of the turbaned heads when not in use had a very quaint effect.

Having explored the ruins of Chitorgarh, we remounted our good elephant, which waited for us, and descended, moving rather joltingly down the long hill, and frightening a pony and a camel tethered in the main street of Chitor. The sun was now blazing, it being noontide, though tempered by the still cool wind from the north, which we had found really cold in the morning.

Returning the way we had come to our quarters at the station, after taking tiffin at the bungalow we arranged to go on to Udaipur in the morning, and were advised to sleep in the train, which waited in the station all night, and left at 6.20 A.M. for Udaipur. So we packed up and went on board and took our berths, which were on the whole more comfortable than the station beds.

In the morning our compartment was invaded by a young Indian who wanted a seat, but we had kept it to ourselves during the night, which was cold enough, and we were glad of all our wraps. The young Indian was a pleasant, bright, and intelligent young fellow who spoke English well, well clad in the style of a native gentleman, with plenty of wraps and overcoats. He was obviously curious about us, and wanted to know all we would tell him. He seemed to have a great wish to see London, and asked us about the cost of living there, and whether a Hindu could live there according to his religion without meat. He described India as "a poor country," and wondered that we should journey so far to see it. He was bound for some town where his father lived, sixty miles by tonga from Udaipur, being under orders not to stop at the latter place, as his father had told him there was plague there, and wished him to come on.

The train passed through a very flat and rather cheerless country, exceedingly dry, and for the most part covered with long jungle grass, but varied here and there by green crops under irrigation.

Camels were occasionally seen, generally ridden by two men; also there were many herds of oxen and buffaloes. As usual, there were many interesting types and groups to be observed at the stations.

Approaching Udaipur, the country broke into hills and became more interesting. We reached Udaipur Station about 11.30, and bidding good-bye and exchanging cards with the young Hindu, we parted with our baggage into a little open cart called a "tum-tum," and were driven some distance, along a dusty road, to the Udaipur Hotel, which looked like an expanded bungalow with a second storey added on. Here we found pleasant quarters and decent beds.

At the table-d'hôte there was a rather frigid Anglo-Indian family, a colonel on a tour of official inspection and his secretary and their ladies; also a voluble American lady, whom we had seen at Ajmir, and a rather lofty and superior English military man and his wife, who, we were afterwards informed, were the guests of the Maharajah.

In meeting one's compatriots aboard or indeed anywhere without an introduction one is reminded by their manner strongly of the Oxford Don who could not do anything to save an unfortunate undergraduate from drowning because "he had not been introduced."

Here, in a remote part of India, chance had thrown half-a-dozen English people together at the same table, and yet they would hardly speak to each other, that is to say to any new-comer outside their own party. Nothing, however, daunts the American traveller, especially the American lady. She ignores the social ice, or if she perceives it she boldly breaks it with a hatchet, as it were, rushing in under the guns of the most frigid and unapproachable personalities with a cheerful and persistent fire of conversation, popping in leading questions with the most artless and childlike confidence. This mode of attack generally succeeds, too, apparently. I have seen severe English official and military-looking men, after some show of resistance, unconditionally surrender, and presently empty their intellectual pockets on the demand of these light-hearted, table-d'hôte, globe-trotting inquisitors.

A picturesque feature of hotel life in India is the impromptu bazaar formed under the arcade, which always shades the rooms on the ground floor, by the travelling merchants, who spread out their wares to tempt the traveller.

In Rajpootana, the land of warriors, collections of arms, swords, sword-sticks, knives and daggers, and fearsome and wonderful blades of all sorts form a conspicuous part of the stock-in-trade of these native merchants, the glittering steel making a brave show with the bright-coloured stuffs, jewellery, and embroideries. At Udaipur they offered also native pictures, painted in tempera, somewhat crude but distinctly decorative, and complete with painted borders or frames. They represented elephants, tigers, maharajahs sabring wild swine, and such-like, painted in profile in frank flat colours, the

RAJPUTS AND THEIR RARITIES. (UDAIPUR)

animals singularly faithful in silhouette to nature. In dealing with these travelling traders, bargaining is, of course, expected, and usually they are willing to accept about half the price originally asked.

An impressive sight at Udaipur is the place of tombs, or the burning-place, which is a beautiful garden surrounded by a high wall, full of magnificent domed tombs and cenotaphs. This is the place where the Kings of Udaipur, since it became the capital of Rajpootana, have been buried, or rather cremated, with their wives. The city of Udaipur —a glimpse of which, with its crenellated walls and the huge pile of the Maharajah's palace rising above the trees, is seen from the hotel—is entered, after a short drive through a fine double gateway. A huge old mango tree grows over the street just inside. Udaipur is a white town ; the streets are very picturesque, having arcaded bazaars and pretty fantastic balconies here and there, and the native life is of course very varied and full of colour. The main street rises up to the eminence on which the palace stands. At an angle before this is reached, a steep flight of white steps leads up to the gate of the court of the great temple of Juggernath —a Jain temple dedicated to Vishnu—the second person in the Hindu Trinity. It was the finest of its kind we have yet seen. We were allowed to walk around the court and examine the carvings, but not inside the temple. Two great stone elephants stand facing one another at the entrance to the court—a similar arrangement to that noted at Ellora. There is an elaborate shrine over the gateway in which is a seated bronze or brass figure of Vishnu with his lotus flower, snakes, and other emblems. The exterior of the temple is a wonderful mass of carving. On the plinth was a continuous narrow frieze of elephants on a small scale, having the effect of a richly carved moulding ; above this was a line of horses, all saddled and bridled but without riders ; above this again was a band of human figures. Over these were carved on a larger scale a series of figures of dancing-girls in different attitudes. These dancers always form an important element in the carved decoration of Jain temples.

We next visited the palace of the Maharajah, which occupies the highest ground in the city of Udaipur. It is a vast, romantic-looking pile. The steep street leads the traveller up to a great arched gateway, and through this is entered a large oblong court. On the right, the vast white palace walls rise to a great height, with hardly any windows, but high up are seen fairy-like arcades, balconies, and domed minarets, glittering with blue tile-work and gold.

A native custodian conducted us over the Palace. Entering an inner court, we ascended a steep stone staircase at an angle, the treads rising about nine or twelve inches high. There were native paintings on the walls of richly caparisoned state elephants bearing maharajahs, tigers, and other figures. We passed through a succession of rooms and courts at different levels, the walls of white marble inlaid with a very fine sort of glass mosaic, not tessellated but let in in pieces cut large or small according to the forms to be expressed. These were generally figures always in severe profile, in elaborate costume, and jewels the details of which were carefully and richly rendered. Flowers and delicate palm trees varied the designs, done in the same way, the leaves and small component parts being cut complete in the glass. There were also formal floral borders outlining the arches of the arcades, and forming ceiling patterns in some of the rooms, and on the walls were hung in frames delicate paintings on vellum, heightened with gold, such as one sees in old Indian illuminated MSS. In some of the corridors it was rather a shock to see inserted in the windows pieces of crudely stained European glass, such as were in vogue in conservatories here in the "forties." One room was entirely decorated with coloured glass, the walls being veneered with a zigzag pattern in red and white glass.

Other and smaller rooms in the Zenana quarters, which we had now reached, and all at the top storey of the Palace, were lined with old Dutch tiles, others again with Chinese blue and white tiles. These rooms had graceful, arcaded balconies which commanded extensive views. We had a bird's-eye view of the palace courts and the stable yards, where elephants were tethered in long rows, the busy natives moving about with horses and oxen. Beyond were seen the clustering, small white houses with flat roofs, broken by domes here and there, the green wooded country and the hills far away, while on the other side of the palace the lake with its pavilioned islands mirrored the sunset framed in the blue mountains.

At night we frequently heard the weird cries of the jackals which prowl around most places in India after dark, and when all is quiet in human habitations. It is a very wild, shrill sound, rising almost to a shriek at times. We also thought we caught another note—the laughter of the hyena.

A charming excursion by boat may be made to the palace of Jagmandir, which occupies the whole of an island on the lake, a fairy-like pavilion enclosing luxuriant palms and fruit trees within its

THE MAHARAJAH'S PALACE AT UDAIPUR. FROM THE JAGMANDIR PAVILION

courts and gardens in which one realised the architecture and scenery of the Arabian Nights.

We reached the lakeside through a fine triple-arched gate which led to a flight of steps descending into the water. Here a striking scene burst upon us. A crowd of dark Hindu women thronged the steps, clad for the most part in rich red saris of different tones, varied by orange and purple drapery and the glitter of their silver bangles and anklets. They were busy cleaning their brass water jars, scrubbing and polishing them on the steps at different levels ; some standing in the water, whilst others, filling their vessels and poising them on their heads, would move away stately and erect, like walking caryatids.

Presently a rather heavy boat with two native oarsmen, which had been summoned by our guide moved from the palace to the steps and we, with our bearer, embarked, and were rowed over to the enchanting island and the fairy-like palace of Jagmandir where Shah Jehan lived when in revolt against his father, Jahangir. On the way we rowed around another island showing white arcades and domes emerging from green bowery foliage of mangoes and palms.

Landing at the steps we found the Jagmandir a most lovely place, full of arcaded courts, and marble pavements, pointed windows and balconies and marble walls enclosing green gardens full of roses, and palms, and plantains, a kingly pavilion, displaying all the invention and refinement of Môgul art. Inside, too, the palace was full of interest. There was a charming little painted chamber, the walls treated in a sort of tapestry manner with Indian scenes and decorative landscapes rich with trees and varied with all the characteristic birds and animals (the white cranes on the mango tree which we had seen in reality at Ahmedabad were there) kites and crows, and antelopes, and the Maharajah and his horsemen hunting the tiger amid these painted forests and jungles. On one wall the Maharajah himself was painted at full length in profile in a white turban and dress also white embroidered with gold, with a gold nimbus about his head as he is supposed to be descended from Rama, and is considered a sacred person connected with the sun—a large sun face modelled and guilded appears on the palace wall.

Another room was said to have been painted by a French artist. He had taken the lotus as a motive and had tuned it into a formal scroll pattern in the frieze, but it was not a success, and had not the interest or the spirit or decorative instinct of the native artist.

The chief salon had Parisian carpets on the floor, and a dreadful blue glass chandelier, and other horrors in glass and furniture of Western origin. Opening out of this salon was a bedroom raised a step or two on a higher level and the principal feature here was a large bedstead in glass and silver! On the walls of one of the courts was a decoration in gesso inlaid with glass, which was both delicate and effective. There were figures decoratively treated in severe profile, combined with trees and flowers somewhat Persian in feeling and similar in style to some we had seen in the Maharajah's palace.

From the landing-place I made a sketch of that palace in the sunlight reflected in the calm waters of the lake. Then, at noon we rowed back to the town and returned in our tonga to the hotel.

Another of the sights of Udaipur is to see the Maharajah's wild pigs fed. He has an arena near the town for the cruel sport of pig-sticking, but keeps vast herds of pigs upon the mountain sides at the head of the lake. It is a beautiful drive to the spot through the city and out at a further gate, and through groves and along a terrace-like road by the lakeside, to a white building on a high ground overlooking the wooded and rocky mountain side, partially covered with low forest; there from a terrace we could see many swine feeding. They are like a small kind of wild boar, but differing in size, and very fierce, bristling their backs and charging one another over the food, which was Indian corn, scattered broadcast among them by two natives, one carrying the sack of grain and the other distributing it from a sort trencher. There was a sort of Brobdingnagian mouse-trap on the ground, presumably to catch the boars in, when wanted for the arena. There were but few boars at first to be seen, but they seemed to know the feeding time, and gradually gathered in large numbers, and when the grain was scattered, by their constant rushes after it and violent charges with each others soon raised such a thick cloud of dust that they became lost to view as in a thick mist, and could only hear their hoofs scraping over the rocky ground, and their savage grunts and squeaks. A number of peacocks hovered on the outskirts on the look out for stray grain as well as blue rocks and crows which often perched on the hogs' backs! The terrace from which we surveyed this strange scene was really the parapeted flat roof of the keeper's dwelling. A flight of steps led up to a higher terrace which surrounded a deep sort of bear-pit, where a select family of hogs seemed to be treated with peculiar distinction. Not for these the fierce struggle for grain upon the mountain side, when the battle was to the strong; no, these were fed upon a special food—a sort of large brown rissole composed of buttermilk and sugar-cane; but the hogs were fat and did not devour these attractive morsels, even with half the zest which their less favoured relatives outside ate up the scattered maize. The reason of the comparative luxury in which these selected hogs lived, we learned, was that they had fought with tigers, and thus were treated as superior beings, by order of the Maharajah.

The wooded shores of the lake and the mountains beyond were very beautiful in the still evening atmosphere, as we drove back to Udaipur, the road by the lake being so narrow that two carriages could not pass, and, meeting the Resident, we had to pull in to one side to let his carriage get by.

There was a charming view of Udaipur from our hotel seen through the trees, the massive Maharajah's palace dominating the city, and bathed in the roseate early morning sunlight it looked particularly lovely. I worked at a sketch of this on Christmas morning; I remember, having to be up at seven o'clock in order to catch the effect, which soon changed. We had the most brilliant moonlight nights here, too.

We visited the Maharajah's gardens where was a sort of Zoo. There were some handsome tigers in rather small cages, hogs, leopards, one lion, deer, guinea-pigs, geese,. cockatoos, and other birds and beasts, including some melancholy dogs of various breeds, chained at intervals around a courtyard. These were supposed to be in hospital.

From the Zoo we drove through a fine wooded park to the Museum called the Victoria Institute, where a native curator showed us round. It was a white building in the Moslem style but quite new. It included a library in which was placed a bad statue of our late Queen. There were modelled heads in coloured plaster, ranged in cases numbered and ticketed, of all the Hindu castes, each with their proper caste mark upon their foreheads. There was a miscellaneous collection otherwise, native arts and industries and antiquities, as well as European, being represented very sparsely. The whole thing had a sort of forced and artificial character in such surroundings and was quite empty of visitors. We were, however, early there.

In driving through the gate of the city, a funeral passed us—a band of young men bearing on a stretcher the corpse which was swathed in red cotton and tightly bound up like a mummy. The bearers moved at a quick, almost jaunty pace, approaching a trot, and with them were other natives who chanted a sort of song. If it was an equivalent for a dirge it was quite a cheerful one —but then the Hindus, as well as the Mahammedans and Indians, look upon death as a happy translation to another existence, and the accompaniments of gloom to which we are accustomed in Christian countries have no existence here.

We departed, on Christmas Day in the morning, from Chitor and Ajmir again, returning by the way we came. Udaipur is at the end of the branch line from Ajmir which has not I believe been in existence many years.

On the way to the station I noticed some very primitive huts clustered in a group on a rising ground above the road. They almost exactly resembled the huts of the early Britons and Gauls as they appear on Trajan's column, being circular in form, built of mud or sunbaked bricks and roofed with a sort of rude thatch laid over a bamboo trellis. In this land of wonders and contrasts truly, one sees everything both in customs and dwellings from the most primitive to the most elaborate and luxurious, from the most ancient to the most modern forms of life. It is sad to note, however, that at least as far as the outward aspects of life are concerned, all that Western contact seems to have done for the people of India is to introduce corrugated iron, Manchester cotton, and the kerosene can—with petrol and its smell!

At Udaipur station there was a great native crowd of every variety of type, wonderful in colour and costume. Many of the men carried sabres as well as walking-sticks which seem to be the marks of superior caste in Rajputana. There were, too, the usual crowd of poorer travellers with their extraordinary bundles and brown babies. A native woman stood on the platform with a huge sheaf of sugar-cane which she sold in pieces to the travellers, and, of course, there were the sweet stuff sellers, and the inevitable betel-nut.

Reaching Chitorgarh in the late afternoon the old fort with its zigzag walled road looked quite familiar, and at the station our elephant was in waiting again.

We could not get on to Ajmir until night, and so did not arrive there until about 5.30 in the morning. Coming from a plague-stricken district passengers were not allowed to leave the train until a medical inspection had taken place. An English doctor with a native attendant bearing a lantern came round and went through the farce of feeling everybody's pulse before anybody was allowed to leave the station. We only stopped, however, to get some tea and await a train for Jaipur, our next destination.

CHAPTER VI

JAIPUR

IN our travels through India we met comparatively few of our own countrymen and women. The English (or the British) have not as yet taken much to touring in the Empire of which such a proud boast is constantly made. The English in India are usually residents connected with civil or military posts. They go out to take up their official duties, and directly they get leave they rush "home"—England is always spoken of as "home," even by residents in India of long standing. It generally happens that the officials and their families are quartered at some particular station in a particular district, and may remain there all their time, so that the English resident in India generally does not see any other parts of the great peninsular, and is not acquainted with the country beyond his own district. A tourist, therefore, in a few months may have a more complete general or even particular acquaintance with India at large, as regards its great cities and famous monuments, than many a resident who has spent the best part of his life in one station, and who always takes his leave at "home."

French tourists are occasionally met with, but Americans are the most numerous, and they are met with everywhere. The early morning train we had taken from Ajmir to Jaipur was invaded by a party of no less than forty of our Transatlantic cousins, who overflowed it and filled our compartment with an incredible amount of hand baggage. They seemed to be, as far as one could make out, connected with some mission. They reminded me rather of a gathering in one of the cities of the United States at which I was present (Philadelphia, I think), where one of my American friends remarked, "Now, all these you see here are types, but none of them are worth studying"!

The country traversed between Ajmir and Jaipur is mostly plain, and very desert-like in places, with distant mountain ranges beyond, not unlike Arizona in general character. Green crops under irrigation are, however, occasionally seen, and among them not unfrequently may be noticed a pair of large, grey-plumaged cranes, feeding in the young corn, which do not take to flight at the approach of the train. We reached Jaipur about noon and put up at Rustom's Hotel, a comparatively short drive from the station. The hotel stands in the middle of a large enclosure divided by a low wall from the high road. Tents are pitched along one side of the building to afford extra sleeping accommodation, and a sort of bungalow annexe is prepared to take overflow guests. From pleasant rooms on the terrace we had a view of the Tiger Fort and the road with its constant procession of natives, ox-carts, and camels and horsemen trooping into the city about a mile off. A row of tall acacia trees screened the late afternoon sun, and 'barred-like fretwork the golden light of afterglow, and we often watched the peacocks flying up to roost among the branches, their beautiful forms silhouetted against the orange sky between the interstices of the leaves.

The native proprietor, or manager, during the preliminary ceremony of taking our names, and in

HOTEL ACCOMMODATION (JAIPUR), "FOR YOUR EASE AND COMFORT" (OR RATHER FOR THE EASING OF YOUR RUPEES ?)

getting a form of application to the Resident filled up for permission to visit the Maharajah's palace and the palace at Amber, made polite speeches, expressing himself only anxious for "our ease and comfort"—of course without any thought of prospective rupees. Clusters of native huts built of mud with thatched roofs occur at frequent intervals around Jaipur outside the city walls; from our terrace at the hotel we could see several. There was apparently a small village within a stone's-throw. One evening the strains of what sounded like a native chant or song in chorus were wafted to us from this village, and we heard that a native wedding was going on there; but the illusion was somewhat destroyed when we learned that the supposed native music proceeded from the mouth of a gramophone! It is said that special ones are now prepared for the Indian market with popular native songs and music—another boon from the West.

Jaipur is a city within high crenellated walls, built of rubble and plastered with cement. The same form of palisade-like battlement crested the walls here as at Chitorgarh, and is the common form in Mogul defensive buildings. Among the native huts which cluster outside the walls, I noticed some of wicker; many of the huts, too, had wicker screens—a sort of lattice-work made of bamboo—covering the otherwise open fronts.

Jaipur is known as the rose-coloured city. The Maharajah must be very fond of pink, in fact he may be said to have "painted the town red." The whole of the main fronts of the houses facing the streets are distempered in a kind of darkish rose pink—really red—the rosy hue being largely due to the luminous atmosphere in the full sunlight, and it becomes still rosier in the flush of evening. It is dark enough at anyrate to show a decoration of lines of floral devices and patterns painted in white upon the red walls. The whole scheme, no doubt, was suggested by the red sandstone buildings inlaid with white marble which are the glory of Delhi and Agrá. It is not a sort of imitation calculated to deceive any one, however, but clearly a scheme of painted decoration emulating the effect of the solid materials mentioned. The city has, owing to this treatment, a very distinctive scenic aspect of its own, and is very striking, the brilliant and varied pattern of vivid colour in the costume of the natives in the bazaars, with this roseate background, producing quite a unique effect. One has, however, after a time an impression of unreality and unsubstantiality, as of stage scenery which will presently be shifted. The Maharajah of Jaipur has the reputation of being very advanced and modern in his ideas. He has at anyrate set up gasworks in his city, which also possesses a large public garden laid out in the European manner, and is both horticultural and zoological, and contains a museum and a bronze statue of Lord Mayo.

It seems rather a mistake, in a climate like that of India, to lay out grounds with broad serpentine paths and drives unshaded by trees, and vast lawns which can only be kept up with a pretence of greenness by constant and laborious watering. It is another of the mistaken foreign importations. The Eastern type of garden, on the other hand, is quite appropriate and adapted to the necessities of the climate. Its characteristics are narrow, straight paths between closely planted groves of trees, acacias, plantains, palms, and fruit trees, and varied with tanks and fountains, and cool marble pavilions, the whole enclosed in a protecting wall like an earthly paradise.

It does not cheer the English traveller in the East—at least I never heard that it did—to see a low wall surmounted by a cast-iron railing and common-place but pretentious gates, enclosing a joyless "public garden" of a British vestry type.

The proprietors of the art depots in the bazaars of Jaipur are very enterprising, and resort to all kinds of allurements to induce the traveller to enter and purchase. To begin with, the tourist in his carriage is peppered with a perfect hail of white business cards flung at him by active touts, who are always on the alert for the passing stranger in the bazaars, who receives such seductive invitations as "See my shop?"—"Very nice things"—"Don't want you to buy—only to look!"

We visited a large art-dealer's store. It was prettily arranged around a small covered court, lighted from the top. An arcade divided a series of rooms along each side, both on the ground and on a second floor. This court was richly carpeted and furnished with seats, coffee tables, and divans. One device of the proprietor or manager was to invite prospective customers to witness a dance of nautch girls in this court, presumably to conduce to a favourable mood for extensive purchases.

At this place was a great display of Jaipur enamels, applied in a variety of ways from small jewellery to large, chased, brass dishes and trays. I saw a large dish prepared by the native craftsman (who was sitting at work at the entrance) for champlévé enamel, very deftly chased, though the modern reproductions of the traditional Indian patterns strike one as rather mechanical. The skill of the craftsman is there, but the feeling and initiative of the artist is too often wanting.

Rajput arms and armour hung on the white walls of the court, and there was an immense stock of all sorts of metal-work and jewellery, mostly modern, and numbers of small portable articles in brass, evidently meant for the eye and the pocket of the tourist; amongst these were quantities of small pierced brass boxes in the form of cushions. I saw some interesting old Indian miniature pictures from MSS.—one of a rajah shooting a bow: he was standing upon a globe which rested on the back of an ox, which again stood upon the back of a fish.

There were some suits of chain mail of extraordinary fineness, and wonderful engraved blades of many kinds. Besides the well-known Jaipur enamelled jewellery there was a quantity of precious stones—garnets, amethysts, sardonyx, onyx, and jade. Another speciality of Jaipur work are the charming spherical rolling lamps. These are spheres of brass chased and pierced all over with floral pattern, and made to open. Inside, by a very ingenious bit of mechanism, a small lamp is so suspended that it always maintains a horizontal position, and though the sphere may be rolled along the ground it never upsets the lamp within. They are used in the temples at festival times. These lamps are made at the Art School at Jaipur, where many native handicrafts are practised.

Continuing our drive about the city we were introduced to the Maharajah's state elephant. He was a fine beast, and occupied a low walled court, all to himself and his keeper. His forehead, trunk, and ears were decorated with an elaborate painted arabesque—a pattern in which vermilion, yellow,

THE MAHARAJAH'S STATE ELEPHANT, JAIPUR

and turquoise predominated. His enormous tusks had had their points truncated, and these were tipped and bound with moulded bands of brass. The animal was tethered by one of his hind feet to a post, and stood in the shade of the high palace wall, tranquilly munching stalks of some kind of corn. I reproduce the sketch I made at the time of the elephant and the old man, his keeper.

After tiffin we visited the palace. One could not say much for the taste of some of the decorations. We were shown several large durbar halls with open colonnades, which, however, were closed by hangings, which our guide—a tall, grey-whiskered Rajput—lifted up to show the interiors. The vaulted ceilings were painted with patterns on rather a large scale and in crude reds and blues, rather open and spread out over the white plaster, and somewhat coarse in form. We were then led through the gardens, which were laid out with long tanks with flagged walks each side, lined with gas lamps, but there was no water in the tanks. Farther on we passed through a gateway at the top of a flight of steps to the alligator tank. Here a native attendant having tied a piece of meat to the end of a string, another set up a curious weird call, while yet another ran on to the shore of the lake or tank, and did his best to wake up one or two very torpid alligators which lay in the sunshine by seizing hold of their tails and making them take to the water. Finally, after much persuasion, two alligators were induced to come up for the food. One of these—an old one with no teeth (none of them have tongues)—opened its horrid white mouth and snapped at the piece of meat which the man dangled at the end of the string. Meanwhile big yellow turtles swam up to join in the game, at which they were much quicker than the alligators. Large brown kites, too, seeing what was going on, hovered about expectantly, and dexterously caught fragments thrown to them in mid air. The ubiquitous crow was there also, ready for any unconsidered trifles.

The life of the bazaars at Jaipur is singularly varied and interesting. The streets are unusually wide as native streets go in India. They find room to shake out long strips of newly dyed cotton to dry—a man holding the cloth at each end and waving it wildly about to dry, so that great plashes of yellow or orange and pink are apt to illuminate the streets here and there, as this process is a frequent incident. The brightest red, yellow, green, and blue and pink are also seen in the costumes or rather draperies of the people—the Hindu women in their graceful saris, generally in different shades of red; the Mohammedan women veiling their heads and shoulders in some vivid-coloured muslin—so that one had a general impression of people walking about attired in rainbows. Quaint, two-wheeled vehicles were numerous, often elaborately painted and decorated, called recklas, having awnings over them, and were driven by a superior caste of natives—possibly they might be a sort of equivalent for the gig of respectability which Carlyle writes of. Then there were the heavier ox-carts of the peasant, some of them with a domed cover draped in red within which hidden from view sat the women and children. Another kind of cart was built of bamboo, a curious lattice of the same forming the pole and yoke for a pair of oxen.

Shaving, massage, cleaning teeth, washing, and all the necessary operations, which in the west are generally performed in private, are in Indian native quarters carried on in the open. The natives do not seem to know what privacy is or to feel the need of it. The little naked brown babies everywhere playing freely about are delightful.

Great flocks of pigeons (blue rocks) are always flying about or swooping down to be fed with grain in the open spaces by women ; but they are driven away from the heaps of grain for sale in the bazaars.

The women carry everything upon their heads, and seem to do most of the porterage—bearing endless baskets of brown fuel made in rough flat cakes, bundles of wood, straw, sugar-cane, green stuff, bedding, and water jars. In Rajputana the women wear a rather full skirt under the sari, in many pleats rather after the style of an Albanian fustanelle. Masses of bracelets, some times completely covering their brown arms, are worn, either of coloured glass, or lacquered metal, or silver, and silver anklets as a rule with little bells attached.

Armed horsemen are frequently seen riding in from or out into the country. Elephants, camels, and flocks of goats vary the street scenes, and residents' carriages with outriders ; camels are also sometimes used to draw vehicles, driven in pairs.

Musicians, with the peculiar long handled Indian guitar, jugglers, conjurers, snake charmers, vendors

TO AMBER ON AN ELEPHANT

of stuffs and embroideries, and photograph sellers haunt the open arcades of the hotels and use every device to attract the attention of travellers.

A visit to the deserted city of Amber and its palace is one of the principal excursions outside Jaipur. It is best to start early in the morning, as there is a four to six miles drive by carriage to reach the place whence the ascent to Amber on elephants' backs is made. The road thither takes the visitor through a section of the city of Jaipur, and passes out on the other side into a road skirted with trees and gardens, from amidst which rise the domes of the pavilions of wealthy Rajputs. The Alligator lake is again passed, and some distance beyond this the foot of the hill is reached, when the traveller is expected to leave his carriage and mount one of the elephants in waiting there to take him up to Amber—another two miles.

It is necessary to be furnished with a formal permission from the Resident to visit Amber. Formerly elephants were placed at the disposal of visitors by the Maharajah, but since tourists became numerous elephants must be hired by them. They are by no means richly caparisoned elephants. The housings leave much to be desired, and the seats are much out of repair, and one is lucky to find the foot-board slung at a usable level and fairly horizontal, and if the protecting rail of the seat does not slip out.

For those who are willing to sacrifice processional dignity and spectacular effect, however, as well as a slow shaking, it is quite possible to walk—for the able bodied, and before the sun is high.

After a steepish hill at first the road descends again, and passing along the border of a small lake, turns round at its head and again ascends to the palace on a considerable height, of which a distant view is obtained, as one approaches it, from the road. It is a striking pile of Mohammedan architecture. Three great gateways are passed on the steep approach up the rocky sides of the hill, and the road is protected by a wall, as at Chitorgarh. Finally the great gateway leading into the courtyard of the palace is reached, and we dismount from the elephant and are surrounded by a number of hangers-on, one of which comes forward to act as guide over the palace, which showed traces of considerable restoration. The great doors of solid brass were exceedingly fine (both here and at the Maharajah's palace in Jaipur—really the best things there). There were also doors beautifully inlaid with ivory and ebony to some of the zenana rooms, all the doors being interesting for their woods and joinery. There were some delicate pierced marble screens over the gateway of the inner court which had a most lovely effect seen against the sky. The rooms were very elaborately decorated with a sort of veneer of small pieces of looking-glass arranged in arabesque, and united by cloisonné of gesso forming the lines of divisions of the pattern, similar to that we had seen at Udaipur. This decoration, carried all over a vaulted ceiling, in the sunlight reflected from the floor, glittered like beaten silver. On the lower halls were delicate marble panels of floral designs in relief.

The palace as a whole did not strike us as so beautiful as that at Udaipur, although vastly more so than the Maharajah's at Jaipur.

From the roof and terraces we looked down on gardens and pavilions and on the lake below, then partially dry, and wondered how this vast palace with all its luxurious decoration came to be deserted.

A temple at the main entrance, however, is still maintained for worship, which is that of Kali—one of the aspects or secondary characters of Parvati, the wife of Siva—a savage, blood-thirsty goddess

SHOPPING IN JAIPUR

only propitiated by animal sacrifices. A goat or a kid is still sacrificed daily here. It was pathetic enough to see the innocent, unconscious intended victim—a poor little kid tied at the corner of the platform of the temple by a little heap of sand. Mr W. S. Caine gives a graphic account of how the head of the victim is instantaneously cut off by the officiating priest, an act he witnessed, but we felt no desire to see this execution.

On our way back I saw a curious instance of the boldness of a kite and the unerring way in which they swoop at their prey. A native was walking down the hill in front of us carrying a piece of bread in his hand, from which he ate, swinging it at his side between whiles. A kite hovering above made a sudden swoop at the bread, which he struck with his beak, scattering the crumbs, though he did not succeed in knocking it quite out of the man's hand.

Driving in the evening through the bazaars at Jaipur we stopped the carriage to purchase some native cottons and muslins, and were immediately surrounded by a noisy, struggling crowd of rival traders who filled the carriage with their gay coloured stuffs, and literally covered us up with them. Our bearer negotiated the bargains, and in the end we carried off some characteristic textile souvenirs. On the way back to our hotel we stopped to see the Maharajah's horses, passing through a gateway into a large exercise ground, down the sides of which ran a long open shed, with horses tethered in a line, each horse being secured by long ropes from each hind fetlock fastened to pegs on iron rings fixed in the ground, which sloped down to the open court. In addition to these each horse was tied by a halter, with a rope each side to rings in the manger, and all, of course, had cloths on. There were no partitions between the animals, which I suppose was the reason of their being so carefully secured. There were some very fine animals among them, and the native grooms were very willing to show them off—for a little backsheesh. There were white Arabs, Walers, English hunters, and a tiny Burmese pony.

CHAPTER VII

AGRA

WE left Jaipur for Agra on the 29th of December, finding the usual excited crowd at the station. The train passed through a rather dry, plain country, though varied by crops under irrigation. We changed at a junction named Bandakni, the train we were in going on to Delhi. It was a refreshment station. Here a good tiffin was procurable. Going on about 4.30 in the afternoon, we entered a more fertile and interesting country, the crops being more abundant, and the wells also. There were some fine groves of trees, and distant ranges of hills to be seen. Curious mounds and tumbled boulders varied the plains here and there in places. Peacocks were plentiful, and they even occasionally strayed on to the railway metals at the stations. Antelopes were also to be seen, and once an animal resembling a wolf was seen in the jungle. A jungle, by the way, is not necessarily a slice of tropical forest, full of long grass, tangled creepers, and tigers, but may be any bit of uncultivated country.

We reached Agra about 9 P.M. after a comfortable journey. We put up at the Metropole Hotel—a kind of extended bungalow, with a two-storied centre and two long, low wings of rooms under the usual arcaded arrangement, with a garden in the middle. The rooms were spacious and lofty, but bare, cheerless and cold. The traveller of course must not expect any old-fashioned welcome or personal interest in his comfort or welfare in any country at any modern hostelry in these days. He writes or wires for his room, and he may be thankful if it is ready for him when he arrives. He must be content to be merely No. So-and-so, and may not even see the host or manager at all. There was, naturally, more or less of a rush on Agra about this time, as the preparations for the reception of the Amir of Afghanistan were far advanced, and distinguished visitors were beginning to arrive. The English tourist who had not furnished himself with introductions in such a place was apparently regarded as a mere worm by the superior military and official British circles.

Driving to the fort next morning we were stopped by an English sentry, who produced a written card of Regulations forbidding the entrance of carriages, so we got out and walked through the Emperor Akbar's great Delhi gate (1566), which is on a fine scale, and passed on to the Pearl Mosque, the Moti Musjid, built by Shah Jehan in 1654—the private chapel of the court of the Mogul Emperors—a beautiful white marble building in a fair court. An Arabic inscription records when it was built and why.

We passed on to the great square of the fort which was busily preparing for the reception of the Amir, who was expected to arrive on the 9th of January. They were actually building out an extra portico in solid masonry adding it on to the existing Durbas Hall (Diwan-i-Khas), which was so blocked with workmen and materials it was not possible to see much inside, and our bearer, who was by way of acting as guide when he could, was roughly turned back by an English official. We made the round of the great Akbar's Fort, which is certainly on a noble scale, and returning to the Delhi gate by ugly and mean British barrack buildings, which have been put up within its massive walls, we could not but be struck with the contrast between the work of one Empire and that of another. Over Akbar's great gate, however, floated our Union Flag.

Our next expedition was to the renowned Taj Mahal, the beautiful marble tomb erected by Shah Jehan in memory of his favourite wife, and which was to be his own monument also. The way thither lies through the cantonments and the government gardens. We passed through great encampments, then in a state of busy preparation. On the road was being erected a large triumphal arch in the Moslem style, upon which native workmen were engaged painting and decorating. Native police in khaki and red turbans lined the route at intervals, and saluted as we drove past. The Viceroy's camp was beautifully laid out and arranged with turf, walks, and flowers. We saw a procession of native women carrying palms and plants in pots on their heads, from ox-carts unloading them, for the camp. Camping in India, indeed, seems to be a fine art, and is carried out in every detail with the utmost completeness. In the government gardens the ideas of the English landscape gardener were in evidence. They were laid out with serpentine

AGGRAVATING AGRA

walks and drives in the modern public parks style, the large shadeless stretches of would-be turf struggling to show a little green under repeated waterings, with groups of young trees here and there. A big statue of Queen Victoria was placed conspicuously on the high ground in the centre of one of these desert-like lawns. A little beyond we came to the magnificent gate of the Taj, a noble structure of red sandstone and white marble, approached by steps. Passing through its deep shadow under the great arch the wonderful tomb in all its pearly whiteness, with its graceful dome and slender minarets, rising sparkling in the full sunlight above a green bower of trees against the deep blue of the sky, and reflected in the still water of the long tank, breaks upon the sight like a fairy vision. The tank with terraced walks, flagged with stone, extends from the steps of the entrance gateway to the front of the Taj itself, its long line only broken by a raised marble terrace with seats about half way. Rows of slender cypresses enforce the long perspective which leads the eye up to the shrine. The Moslems certainly felt the importance of spacing and proportion, and the art of leading the eye and preparing the mind for the appreciation of beautiful art and architecture by careful planning of the setting and surroundings of their great temples and tombs. Space is as important an element in their design as the exquisite handicraft which produced their unrivalled detail. The Taj itself is on a raised platform of stone, and is flanked on each side by two noble mosques of red sandstone splendidly inlaid with white marble. It was the rich decorative effect of such materials no doubt which suggested to the Maharajah of Jaipur the painting of his town red, which I refer to in a previous chapter, but the reality compared with the imitation is as wine to water.

THE TAJ MAHAL, FROM THE GATEWAY

The Taj first impresses one by its beautiful proportion, and the completeness of its ensemble. It is like a fair woman whose general carriage and aspect charms the eye before we are near enough to appreciate the full beauty of her face and form, or to note the exquisite taste of her delicate attire.

As one approaches this wonderful shrine which, although so ornate, possesses a fine breadth in general effect, the beauty and finish of its decorative detail excites a new admiration. There are delicate designs of lilies and tulips and crown imperials cut in marble in low relief, forming the panelling of the lower walls. These are framed in small-scale, formal floral designs, inlaid with precious stones, such as jasper, coral, bloodstone, sardonyx, lapis-lazuli, onyx, turquoise, and other kinds done in a manner associated with Florentine work, and it is said Italian workmen were employed here. Then we have the crowning beauty of the pierced work in the marble screens which enclose the tombs, and break the brilliant light at the apertures under the dome. These are the jewellery and lace of this architectural personality. There is something of the fine lady about her—if one may use the personal pronoun, but one cannot forget the twenty thousand workmen whose twenty-two years' toil contributed to her splendour; and it is recorded, too, that their work was done under conditions of semi-starvation, and at the price of many lives, over and above the four millions of money at which the cost is usually estimated. Well, it remains *their* monument as well as that of Shah Jehan and his wife Arjamand

Banu: 1648 is the date of the completion of the Taj.

I was somewhat disappointed not to find the eastern garden described by Edwin Arnold, and which was seen here by Mr W. S. Caine—a bowery, romantic garden full of fruit trees—"orange and lemon, pomeloes, pomegranates, palms, flowering shrubs and trees, with marble fish-ponds and fountains, speaking of the East in every whisper of their leaves and plash of their waters." There is still a charming garden, but an Anglicised one, with open lawns, broken by masses of beautiful and varied but rather consciously and professionally arranged trees and shrubs and palms. The hand and taste of the modern gardener is a little too evident. It looks as if the original somewhat wild and characteristic Eastern garden had been taken in hand by an expert from Kew, and it had been tamed, its wild locks cut off, and the remainder combed and brushed.

There is an English country-seat or even surburban suggestion about it in parts. I cannot but think that it was a pity not to maintain the garden in its Eastern character, considering the monument it encloses. However, it would take even more professional treatment to prevent beautiful trees and flowers from being delightful.

The garden is still a pleasant place to wander in, and interesting views of the white domes and minarets, rising above masses of foliage, can be had everywhere in it. Here, at the end of December, one enjoyed the temperature, and the sunshine, tempered by the shade of trees, of a normal June day in England.

As regards the garden, I was told that when it was in its original state as a fruit garden a certain amount of revenue was realised by the sale of the

THE MAINSTAY OF INDIA. AQUARIUS—THE WATER-BEARER

produce. When Lord Curzon heard of this he considered it not fitting, and I understood that he was responsible for the alteration in the character of the garden, which requires the constant attention of the water-bearer with his goatskin.

Agra possesses a fine mosque in the Jama Musjid, built by Shah Jehan in 1644. It is a building of red sandstone and white marble. The big dome is inlaid in zigzags of white marble and red sandstone alternately, the whole surface being covered in this way with striking effect.

It is an interesting drive through the bazaars and over the bridge of boats across the river Jumna, and through a native village, to the mausoleum of Itmad-ud-Daulat. In this beautiful building, which is approached through a massive arched gateway of red sandstone and across a walled garden, one sees a prototype of the Taj Mahal. In this case there is a central dome and four minarets, only the cupola is lower and of a flatter curve, and the minarets are not detached from the body of the building which is much lower than the Taj. In the design and execution of its decorative detail, however, it surpasses the Taj in inventiveness, and variety and richness, both in pierced and carved work and its *pietra dura*. The detail of the Taj, beautiful and finely finished as it is, has in comparison, perhaps, rather the look of having been done to order, whereas in buildings of earlier date like this one we seem to see the more spontaneous invention of the craftsman. The restoring hand of Lord Curzon, however, has touched this monument also, and a new marble balustrade around the flat roof has been added under his orders. There are lovely views from the minarets.

We visited the Taj Mahal again by moonlight. It was the 30th of December and the moon was full, but it was chilly driving out after dinner and wraps were necessary. There was a light mist from the river which hung over the garden, and slightly veiled the lower part of the building as we approached it down one of the long paths chequered by the shadows of the trees. The front was in shadow and looked mysterious in the mist, but the dome seemed made of pearl rounded in the full moonlight in splendid relief against the dark deep blue of the night powdered with brilliant stars, while the four minarets were like helmeted sentinels in shining armour, guarding the sacred shrine.

The moonlight was bright enough for me to make a sketch by. I also made two coloured drawings of the Taj by daylight, one of which—"the Taj Mahal from the rose garden" was afterwards purchased by H.M. The Queen, and the other, from the gate, is reproduced here. Agra was full of British and native soldiers, and more were continually arriving. We passed trains of field artillery marching through the government gardens, and bell tents covered the ground like mushrooms. In many places earth banks had been cut in tiers for seats, and strings of small flags fluttered across many of the streets, and there were also seats and stands of timber being erected. Agra could think of nothing but the Amir.

The English and other churches are not admirable examples of modern architecture, and never seem to look at home in India. There was a Roman Catholic Church here after the manner of an eighteenth century one, but any merit it might have had was obscured by its colour. It had been, so to speak, put into a grey uniform with buff facings. The English Church was treated in the same way. This must be military influence. My impression certainly was that civilians did not count for much at Agra.

In the bazaars we found we were able to make purchases with rather less accompaniment of drama than at Jaipur. European goods were much in evidence, of the cheap and nasty sort as a rule, ugly socks and scarves and cottons, and tin ware. I saw a crowd of natives clustering round the trumpet mouth of a gramophone—an instrument which seems to have considerable charms for them.

It was chilly enough in the early mornings and in the evenings at Agra, and our ground-floor rooms were none of the warmest, although, of course, the sun was very powerful in the middle of the day. The Hotel proprietors were looking forward to full houses and high prices during the Amir's visit, and enormous sums were mentioned as probable charges for rooms, but we had no intention of staying through the festivities.

Our last excursion from Agra was to Sikandra—five miles away to the North West—where we drove to see the tomb of Akbar. The road was a dusty one, but through pleasant acacia avenues. We passed through several mud-built villages, and presently saw white minorets rising above a belt of trees in the distance. At one part of the road where the square tower of an English Mission Church was seen among trees we were reminded for a moment of a bit of Norfolk, but only for a moment. Soon we reached the great red-stone gateway which was on a splendid scale, and elaborately inlaid with marble, exceedingly fine in style, parts had been restored, and all the four white marble minarets were said to be new and placed there by Lord Curzon, not I presume without good evidence of the former existence of such minarets, but such renewals cannot possess any historic interest and are in doubtful taste. The gate was adorned with Togra and Arabic inscriptions, which, cut in sunk relief in white marble, formed a frame work enclosing panels of larger pattern in marble inlay. Pilasters of red sandstone on the front were in zigzag courses, alternately white and red, like the work on the dome of the Jama Musjid at Agra.

From the gateway a long and broad flagged way, intersected by tanks, led us up to the tomb, across a wide park full of fine trees, tamarinds and mangoes chiefly. Arrived at the great tomb, the cupolas of which we had seen in front of us as we walked, we first entered a sort of hall or atrium with richly decorated roof and walls in coloured plaster, heightened with gold, and with an Arabic text in gold running round the frieze. There were beautiful designs of trees and vines in panels. Parts had been picked out in new gold and colour, at somebody's expense, to bring out the pattern, but the new work looked hard and mechanical though on good lines, and the new gold was staring; the effect of this partial restoration being of course patchy. Still, if such restorations are allowable at all, it is better that they should be frank and make no pretence at being really a part of the original work. It would, however, in this case have been far better to have left it alone, as the old gold and colour still remaining on the walls and vault was rich and deep in tone.

From this hall we entered a small corridor, two

native attendants going before us with lanterns to guide our steps. This passage led into a vast dark domed chamber, in the midst of which was the plain marble tomb of the great Akbar. It was impressive in its simplicity, without any inscription or ornament, the usual narrow parallelogram with a moulded base. One of the men uttered a deep prolonged note like the exclamation Ah! but sustained and dwelling on the A. This was answered by a profound and long-continued echo or reverberation, dying gradually away, caused I suppose by the height and shape of the dome. One might imagine it was the voice of the dead Emperor. After seeing three more tombs, one of which was richly and delicately carved (a lady's), we ascended to the terraced roof, and from there to a second arcaded terrace, from which still a third was reached up steps of ever increasing height in the treads, and finally to a top story, emerging upon a beautiful spacious arcaded court of white marble, but with warm tints in it which made it very much the tone of ivory. There were delicate, pierced, marble screens on each side, through which the evening sun sparkled like gold. In the centre of the court on a raised dais was the second tomb of Akbar, according to the usual Mohammedan custom of placing an upper tombstone to indicate the position of the actual tomb in the vault below. This tomb was most elaborately and delicately carved in white marble, with beautifully designed floral patterns and Arabic texts and borders of scroll work, which were like reproductions in marble relief of the designs in the best type of Persian carpets. The aged native custodians told us that the famous koh-i-noor diamond was once here on Akbar's tomb. It might be interesting to trace its history to its present position.

The foliated cresting of the parapet of this marble court was also delicately carved. Altogether the building was one of the finest things of its type we had yet seen in India. The blend of Hindu construction with Mogul work in the corbelled supports of the minarets was noticeable. These corbels were trebled at the angles, and like most of the building were of red sandstone.

There was a fine view of the country from this highest story of the tomb, and we could even see the white dome of the Taj Mahal five or six miles away. The drive from Agra took about an hour, and the sun had set before we returned.

This being New Year's day Moonsawmy our bearer smilingly came up with an offering—a plum cake with a pink sugared top and "A Happy New Year" on it, as if it had come out of an English confectioner's—and this, too, was accompanied by a garland of yellow and white flowers after the native manner—one for each of us. He said this was customary, and with his good wishes he managed to convey a gentle hint that his "jentilmens" usually made him a little present in return. This rather rubbed a little of the sugar off, but, of course, we did not forget him. He was not a bad servant on the whole, though rather too old and cunning a bird in some ways. He had rather extravagant ideas in ordering carriages, which we afterwards discovered were not totally unconnected with certain commissions extracted from the carriage proprietors. No doubt, however, native bearers regard the European tourist as fair game—it is not unheard of in Europe—and they, like other classes after their manner, lose no opportunity of making the most of the chances of their rather uncertain profession.

CHAPTER VIII

GWALIOR

WE left Agra for Gwalior on the 2nd of January. Departing from Agra Road about 11 in the morning we arrived at Gwalior between 3 and 4 o'clock in the afternoon. We hoped to meet an Indian friend here, who was a doctor in the suite of the Maharajah, and whom we had known in London when he was studying for his degree. He was, however, absent at Calcutta, so we had to shift for ourselves. There was, however, an excellent guest-house built by the Maharajah for the use of visitors to Gwalior, not far from the station, where we found comfortable quarters, very superior to most of the hotels we had had experience of. The building itself was a charming pavilion in the Mogul style, with domes, arcades, and pierced stone work balconies, and elaborately carved doorways, the material of which it was built being a sort of yellow sandstone. We were allotted a spacious room opening on to a pleasant terrace and connected with balconies which extended entirely around the house, and from here we could see the famous Rock of Gwalior with its fort and Temples and the old palace of Man Mandir conspicuous at its further end. There was a large central hall or living room, and in this was a blazing fire which shed its cheery light and welcome warmth. There was a good piano and English furniture. There was a sort of clerestory high in the lofty wall, but no direct light, so that in the daytime this room was in comparative gloom, by no means ungrateful after the glare of the sun. The dining room was fully lighted and opened on to a portico. In front of the building was a garden with a rather burnt up piece of lawn encircled by a carriage drive.

We found a singular silent and reserved company of Anglo-Indians at dinner—a lady and three gentleman—only one of the latter manifesting the slightest interest in us. No one appeared at breakfast the following morning but an English governess and a child she was in charge of.

We started in a carriage to drive to the fort, stopping on the way to see the tomb of Mohammed Ghaus, the dome of which is visible from the guest-house. It is a noble tomb of yellow sandstone, with fine screen-work. It dates from the early part of Akbar's reign. We crossed a river by a bridge and entered a decayed-looking native town, passing up a straggling street of low houses to the first gate of the fortress. There we might have hired an elephant to take us up the steep road to the fort, but the elephant had been already bespoke by a party of British officers. A palanquin (or jhampan) was produced, however, in which my wife seated herself and was carried up the hill by four bearers, four more accompanying them as relays. As for me I preferred to walk up, and our Moonsawmy went with us. We passed through several gateways. The Hindu carvings of one called the Ganesha Gate had been defaced by the

TO GWALIOR FORT BY PALANQUIN

Mohammedans. Soon the towers of the old palace of Man Mandir rose in view near the summit, each crowned with a circular cupola. It is a striking building of remarkable character in reddish-yellow sandstone, faced in parts by turquoise blue and yellow tiles, courses of these tiles running across the façade. The angle tower and some of the tile-work at the top had been restored. There was a frieze of geese in yellow on a turquoise-blue ground, the birds in profile, each showing an expanded wing and set close together. The design resembled the carved figures of birds often seen on the Jain temples. The architecture here being Hindu, was much more massive than the Mogul work hitherto seen, and showed much variety and invention in the carved corbels and brackets in the interior. I made a note of a peacock bracket in which the tail is effectively treated, the bird being considerably formalised in adapting it to its architectural purpose. There was another of a fantastic elephant. Elephant heads with their uplifted trunks, by the way, were carved as brackets to support the balconies at the Guest House, where also I noted that the detail of some of the carved work of the door heads at the old palace had been reproduced. The doorways were rather low and small, and the whole building had more the character of a castle than a palace. On the flat table land on the summit of the rock there were several Jain temples, masses of carving within and without. The Sas Bahu is the principal Jain temple, and there is also a Hindu temple on the rock—near the farther end from Man Mandir—the Teli-ka Mandir. This stands in a graveyard, full of carved fragments and upright stones. The elephant bearing the party of British officers passed us as we were exploring the temples. There are some ugly barracks, which are very much out of keeping with the historic architecture of the Rock. The old fort has stood many a siege. Caine calls it "the cockpit of Central India," and "it has been stormed or starved into submission a dozen times at least." It seems to have been originally fortified in 773 A.D., and at various periods since to have alternately fallen into the hands of Hindu or Mussulman, as now one and now the other prevailed. Akbar the Great took it in 1556, and we find the East India Company in possession in 1780, who took it from Sindhia and gave it to the Rana of Gohad. Then Sindhia retook it, and so it has remained with the Sindhias (to which family the present Maharajah belongs) practically ever since. The Rock has always been well supplied with water and has many tanks.

We had a commanding prospect of the country, stretching in a vast plain for miles around. We could see the Maharajah's palace amidst its parks and gardens—a white building among the green foliage, and nearer the foot of the Rock the new town of Gwalior, called Lashkar. We descended on the farther (northern) side of the rock by a winding road, and from here we saw some huge carved figures cut in the face of the sandstone cliffs in bold relief. Most of these are said to represent Adinath, the first Jain pontiff, but there is a seated figure of Nemnath, the twenty-second pontiff. Each bear their symbols, that of the first being a bull and of the second a shell. There are life-size as well as small figures cut on the lower parts of the cliff. The effect of these strange carvings is very weird. They have an impersonal and unrelated look, and give one the impression of being more ancient than they really are; but they only date from A.D. 1441 to 1474.

We found our carriage waiting for us at the foot of the hill, having driven round the Rock from the old town, and we got back to the Guest House about noon.

In the late afternoon we drove to the Maharajah's palace, and presenting our cards, were shown over the rooms by a very polite English officer. The building is in a sort of late Italian Renaissance style, all white outside, with a great display of pilasters and columned porticoes. We entered a vast durbar hall in white and gold, with modern French-looking furniture with curly legs upholstered in green. There were many photographs of recent English Governor-Generals on the walls, as well as indifferent full-length, life-sized portraits in oil of the late Maharajah. The best of these was said to have been painted by one Scott—a landscape painter (!). In one of the smaller rooms there was an English water-colour drawing of Sussex Downs by A. F. Grace (whom I remember at Heatherly's in student days), and several photographic official groups of the usual type, in which the Maharajah is seated by the Prince of Wales, surrounded by rows of officials and notabilities, all with "eyes front." We wrote our names in the visitors' book, and then drove through the grounds, which are very extensive. In one part lions are kept—apparently in a most insecure way, as they not unfrequently escape and ravage the country round. In fact, this had quite recently happened, and natives had been killed by them. A very taciturn gentleman at the Guest House had been pointed out to us by the more genial of our fellow-countrymen there as the official who had been sent by the Maharajah to fetch the wandering lions back, and he had been over a distance of about three hundred miles before he succeeded in "rounding them up." He did not tell us, however, how it was done, though he had a look as of one who "could a tale unfold"—not to speak of a lion's tail! When we saw the place where these lions were kept we were not surprised that they should have been able to escape if they had a mind to. We looked down on them as they were gnawing some bones. They were loose in a sort of open court, overgrown with grass, and enclosed within four plastered walls which any cat could have scaled, no palisading or iron railing at the top. There were five lions and one lioness visible. The remains of their repast of meat was pounced on by kites and crows with much clamour.

We next saw the Maharajah's elephants, and passed down a long line of them, chained by the fore-legs, down one side of an open courtyard, all eating what looked like the stalks of Indian corn. There were about thirty elephants here. One of them was handsomely painted on the forehead in a similar way to the state elephant we saw at Jaipur, but none of them had quite such big tusks. Returning through the gardens, we passed the older palace; also a white building, but in the Mogul style, with many domes and minarets, and facing a large tank with marble steps.

Our party at the Guest House was increased at dinner by two very pleasant American ladies, who, owing to their powers of conversation, caused the very reserved Anglo-Indians to melt a little and show some signs of human interest, especially when one of the ladies related her thrilling experiences during the San Francisco earthquake.

The next morning we visited the newer city of Gwalior, which we had seen from the fort. The streets were fairly wide, and some had varied and picturesque fronts in plaster-work. We were driven to the gate of a big and rather new Hindu temple, spoiled by the insertion of crude pieces of coloured glass, of the commonest European make, in the fan-lights of the doors on each side. A sacred bull of black marble and a snake fetish were the most interesting things there.

In the same court was an older temple raised on a flight of steps. To approach this, one's shoes had to be taken off, and from the door only a peep was allowed into the dark interior, which, as far as I could see was painted all over with figures of deities and emblems in a barbaric way in coarse and crude colours. The thing to look at, it appeared, was a portrait of the late Maharajah in his jewels, on what we should call the high altar, which was suddenly illuminated by artificial light by one of the native attendants.

Zebu cows were wandering freely about in the court of the temple, and here for a wonder no fees were taken.

We went into the new market, which had been opened by the Prince of Wales on his visit the

IN THE BAZAAR, GWALIOR

previous year. It was not, however, very busy, and many of the stalls were empty. It seemed of doubtful advantage to the natives, who preferred to do business in the bazaars. There appeared to be a good supply of fresh vegetables, but very few buyers. The most interesting stalls were those of the bead sellers. There were beads of every variety of colour and size. The stalls were about the height of ordinary shop-counters, and on these platforms, which extended without divisions along the centre and sides of the market hall, the native traders squatted with their wares in front of them, women as well as men. Some of them were engaged in stringing the beads, and one man was plaiting a cord, the strands of which were fixed to a hook fixed on an upright stick supported on a stand. He used his toes like fingers to hold out and divide the strands as he worked. With the assistance of our bearer we made some purchases, and again later in the bazaar, when, as the carriage was stopped, I made a sketch of the scene in front of us, but under difficulties, as we were immediately surrounded on all sides by an eager concourse of swarthy, interested spectators, who refused to budge in spite of the rather mild remonstrances or commands of a native policeman, who, I imagine, used the Hindu equivalent for "Pass along" or "Move on," but they didn't. Under this "crowd of witnesses" I endeavoured to complete my sketch, and then we moved on.

Extending our drive on the Morar Road, we passed the camp of the Maharajah's soldiers in waiting for the Amir's coming, as after the Agra reception was over he was to pay a visit to the palace at Gwalior for tiger-shooting. We enjoyed a quiet life at Gwalior, and I was able to make several drawings unhindered by too curious crowds. The Guest House was one of the quietest places imaginable, although visitors came and went and even motor-cars were seen. There was something almost mysterious in the way guests would appear and disappear—at table one day and vanished the next; covers would be laid too for guests who never appeared.

Tents which were pitched on the ground outside the Guest House for other unseen visitors would be clean gone as we looked out in the morning. Everything seemed so transitory; even a native boy, when I wanted to make a drawing of him, was nowhere to be found, and I had to make the best of it with an unwilling and quite inferior substitute, who had no idea of keeping still, and even ended the seance by squatting on the ground with his back to one!

It struck me that the natives do not like being drawn or painted, as a rule, to judge by the various attempts one made to secure models. The one wanted always disappeared when the time came, and another, but not a better and without the same characteristics, offered.

The little palm squirrels were very numerous here, and would scamper about the terraces and balconies of the Guest House, and even chase each other into our rooms, or come up for the crumbs we scattered, sitting up on their haunches to nibble at them, held in their fore-paws in true squirrel fashion. Equally familiar were the sparrows which flew in and out, unmolested and fearless, even perching sometimes on the breakfast table. The crows too would congregate on the balcony rails if

CALLERS AT THE GUEST HOUSE, GWALIOR

any feeding was going on, frequently joining us at afternoon tea, at a respectful distance, though within short range of the scattered crumbs.

We witnessed several very lovely sunsets over the Rock of Gwalior, a type of frequent occurrence being an arrangement of long, low stratus clouds, brilliantly illuminated on their under edges as the sun sank below the horizon, the light deepening from orange into crimson. Another type consisted of golden fleeces of high cirrus clouds, rippling out over spaces of turquoise.

We paid another visit to the old town of Gwalior and climbed the hill as far as the third gate, where I made a sketch showing the towers of the Man Mandir Palace through the arch.

From a terrace extending along the hill near this gate there is a fine panoramic view, the old town lying below, partly ruined and deserted, a mass of crumbling walls and complicated roof plans mingled with trees and gardens.

The first gate at the foot of the hill, where is the guard-house, is interesting as showing the inlaid enamelled tile-work which decorates it partially. Deep turquoise is the prevailing colour, and it is used for the field or background of the designs, and is inlaid in pieces cut to fit the interstices of the pattern in the yellow sandstone. In a frieze of geese in close formal procession, the birds were cut in sunk relief, and the spaces between were filled with turquoise pieces. The tile decoration on the Man Mandir Palace has been done in the same way, yellow and green tiles being also used.

We drove through the bazaar of the old town, a queer, half-ruined, and ragged place, but exceedingly picturesque, the natives squatting on their stalls, presiding over curious preparations of food and other wares, with chatting, many-coloured groups crowding around. Some of the people would look curiously at us, some would salaam, some were indifferent, others were derisive or sullen.

There was rather an important-looking mosque

APPROACH TO THE PALACE OF MAN MANDIR, GWALIOR

with minarets in the town, but many of the houses were roofless and deserted.

In crossing the bridge over the river we noted the people washing clothes, and a pretty pattern of colour was formed when the stuffs were spread out over the sandbanks to dry. Here, in central India, we were able to see more of the everyday life of the people, and had more opportunities of quiet observation of country life than usual. The peasants did not seem to have the curiosity of the natives in the towns, when one sat down to make a drawing; but they went on their way, bearing their burdens, or driving ox-carts, or herds of goats, or buffalo cows, or asses.

It was quite a change to get a grey cloudy effect which occurred one morning when I had found an interesting subject by the river-side. On the way thither we passed a village burning-place, strewn with heaps of ashes where the dead had been burned. The river had shrunk to a small, shallow stream, and at the spot where I sat was crossed by stepping-stones, over which groups of natives constantly passed to and fro. Cattle and ox-carts splashed through a shallow ford at intervals, and higher up natives bathed their brown bodies in the water. We were on the outskirts of the old town of Gwalior, and could see above on the rock the dark shapes of the Jain temples looming up against the sky, while around us were domes of cenotaphs, fragments of tombs, and broken walls, overshadowed by groups of fine banyan trees and mangoes. At an old draw-well near by groups of native women were continually coming and going, bearing their water-jars on their heads, their draperies forming delightful schemes of colour.

A dark thin Hindu in a white turban and waist-cloth was ploughing up his small patch of land near the river for potatoes, which members of his family working with him were preparing to sow. There were several sons—youths—two women, and some small children, all working on the land.

I made a note of the plough, a very primitive implement, having a single shaft fixed at a right angle to the share, with a cross-handle at the top. This the ploughman held with one hand—his left—guiding the plough, while with his right he drove a small pair of zebus under a yoke, who dragged it along. The share was a wedge-shaped piece of wood, tipped with iron at the point and along its edge.

Moonsawmy talked to the man while I made my notes, and he told me afterwards that the ploughman never managed to earn as much as 200 rupees in the year, though he and his family—I suppose about ten or a dozen all told—were constantly at work. His patch of land being near the river, one would have thought favourable for raising crops; but it appeared the river not infrequently was completely dry, and they were hard put to it for water for the soil. The income of the whole family worked out at about thirteen pounds a year at the most, which, taking into consideration that it had to be the support of about a dozen people, seemed narrow enough, and one could easily understand that the slightest failure of the crops would mean something like famine.

This state of things bears out the estimates of the average income of the Indian ryot, calculated by the late William Digby, C.I.E., after long residence and experience in India, the results of whose study of the question are given in detail, from undisputed authorities, in his striking work, "Prosperous British India," in which is accumulated an appalling mass of evidence, all pointing to the conclusion that for famine should very largely be read *poverty*, which is also the root cause of bubonic plague. The railways, of course, might convey corn to the starving districts, but where the people have no money to pay for it they must starve all the same, Government relief-works being the only alternative; but this sort of relief must often be too late for poor creatures reduced by hunger and too weak to work.

The ordinary unprejudiced observer is naturally inclined to ask, Why this desperate poverty in an industrious population, supposed to be under beneficent British rule and administration? The answer must be sought in the fact that thirty millions and upwards are annually extracted from the country without any equivalent return, and this must necessarily mean a heavy burden of taxation on the chief sources of wealth, land and labour.

One of the greatest principles of our Constitution of which our public men are never tired of boasting is, "No taxation without representation," or, "Taxation and representation must go hand in hand." This principle is, however, entirely ignored in India, where British rule is as autocratic as that of

Russia. Is it surprising in these circumstances that there should be "unrest"?

The educated Hindu or Mohammedan—the many who come to England and are trained in English Universities, or read for the Bar, or study for their degrees in medicine, feel that there is no part or lot for them in the administration of the affairs of their own country except in a very subordinate way. I understand that the highest Government post a native can attain to is the office of assistant-commissioner.

Time was when, after the great upheaval of the Mutiny—which was really an attempt to regain possession of the reins of government by the native princes of Oude, the principle of native representation under British administration was advocated by leading English politicians. Nothing, however, came of it, and the policy of the India Office has remained unchanged through all the changes of party government, there being no difference in this matter between Liberals and Conservatives. A Liberal like Mr John Morley, when in office as Indian Secretary, promptly orders the arrest and deportation without trial of Indian agitators under an old law of the East India Company which has never been ratified by the English Parliament.

Mr Laipat Rai, however, appears to be a self-sacrificing and devoted advocate of the cause of his people, and as editor certainly cannot have written so strongly against the English Government as Mr H. M. Hyndman, who has for years past denounced the conduct of the India Office, while challenging attention to and redress of the system under which the people of India are impoverished.

The attenuated ploughman who has been the occasion of these remarks was a typical figure. Looking on such figures, able only to secure a bare subsistence, so common throughout India, one cannot but feel that all the magnificence and luxury of the Maharajahs, as well as the heavy burden of the cost of the British Government, is maintained by the sweat of the brows and the ceaseless toil of such as these.

CHAPTER IX

DELHI

AFTER a stay of about a week at the Guest House at Gwalior we took the road again, or rather the railroad, Delhi being the next place on our itinerary. We thought, however, to break the journey for a few hours at Agra, and get a view of the entry of the Amir, which was fixed for the 9th of January.

It was a lowering, cloudy morning when we left our quarters and made for the railway station, where we had a long wait in the darkness. An enormous throng of natives filled the platform, squatting on the ground or standing about in groups, talking or sleeping under covers which hid them from head to foot. Most were closely wrapped up about the shoulders, cloths being wound over the turban, even so that they had generally a top-heavy look with bare legs. Their wraps were only of cotton though, as a rule, and did not seem adequate against the chill of the morning. One little swarthy man was busy writing, making entries on sheets of paper or perhaps bills of lading. He squatted on the platform against one of the piers of the arcade, writing by the aid of a lantern's light. I noticed only one European besides ourselves in the throng, and he appeared to be an English official and wore a pith helmet.

At last up came the train from Jhansi, and we got in, a slumbering English officer occupying one of the berths. The sky, which was the only gloomy and threatening one we had experienced in India, and certainly looked leaden and hopeless enough, soon turned to rain, and under such an aspect the country looked desolate in the extreme. The tawny earth and fuzzy, dry grass, sparse trees of prickly acacia and scrub bushes, the broken hillocks and mounds of clay, looked more fruitless and forlorn under the steady, soaking rain; groups of poor country folk in their thin cotton clothing huddled together, waiting at the stations we passed, or could be seen splashing through the muddy pools to catch the train.

Nearing Agra, we saw heavy artillery trains with field guns trailing along the wet roads. Troops had been pouring into Agra for some time, and while at Gwalior a native regiment of cavalry (lancers) rode by the Guest House, preceded by their baggage on mules and camels.

At Agra Road Station the rain was pouring in torrents. There is an immense, long, exposed platform, along which we made our way to cover under the station shed, which was already crammed with people, mostly English and American visitors, army officers, and officials.

The weather being quite hopeless, we gave up the idea of seeing anything of the procession, which of course was a military one, and then finding there was a dining-car in waiting, we had a scamper through the rain again down the platform to reach it.

After tiffin we were just in time to catch a train on to Delhi—in fact it had actually started, but the courteous station-master sent an official to stop it

A DASH FOR THE DINING-CAR AT AGRA ROAD

for us, and to see us safely in with our baggage. It was now nearly noon, but our train, a slow passenger one, was not due at Delhi until 5.30. The rain continued steadily, and damp groups of natives were gathered at the different stopping stations in various stages of discomfort. They did not, however, appear to mind the wet so much as one would have expected, but swathed themselves in all sorts of curious wraps up to the eyes, leaving the legs and feet bare, and some even squatted on the wet ground.

The country was again a plain for the most part, and extensively cultivated under irrigation, several irrigation canals being crossed by the railway. Green crops of young corn seemed almost hidden by charlock, the yellow fields having almost the effect of our buttercup meadows in May. Flocks of black and white cranes were seen, as well as a large, blue, grey-plumaged kind, which are usually seen in pairs in the green corn. Three superior-caste Hindus got into our compartment and occupied the cross-bench at one end. One had a bad cough, but they kept their windows open and did not seem to mind draughts. Coughs and throat troubles seemed, indeed, too common in India, and we often heard distressing coughs in the hotels at night.

The sky towards evening began to clear in the west, the whole solid field of rain cloud gradually lifting like a curtain, and the sun shining out while the rain continued, a brilliant rainbow appeared as if painted on the black wall of cloud to the eastward.

The line passes through a part of old Delhi, a vast region of broken tombs and ruined walls lying outside the walls of the present city, and afar off we could see the domes and minarets of the Great Jama Musjid Mosque.

We got in in good time, and collecting our heavy

baggage sent on from Gwalior, drove to Maiden's Hotel, through streets dark with rain and standing in pools of water, a stormy orange sunset casting a warm glow over everything. The hotel was on the usual Indian plan, with a centre and two arcaded wings enclosing a court, along which a series of ground-floor, bungalow-like bed- and bath-rooms extended, chilly enough at this time of year in the mornings and evenings, especially in wet weather. The hotel itself was under English management, and there were large open fires in the dining-room and salon, which looked comfortable, and the cookery was superior to most of the others we had experienced. Letters from England awaited us, and added to our satisfaction. No doubt the mails are delivered with wonderful regularity, and so long as the traveller can arrange his tour in order that his letters shall meet him at certain places, and does not leave before the mail arrives, no complications occur. It is only when letters follow one about instead of preceding one that delay and difficulties occur.

The next morning (January 10) was grey, chill, and damp, when we started after breakfast to see Delhi. The hotels and the British residential quarter lie quite outside the native town, as is usually the case, amid spacious, park-like grounds, here pleasantly undulating, and varied with gardens and fine groups of trees. The town is walled, and has a broad dry ditch as a farther defence. We drove through the famous Kashmir Gate, renowned for the British assault at the time of the Mutiny, which remains in the battered condition in which it was left after the siege, with great shot-holes in its masonry, as well as in the walls each side. A tablet records the circumstances of the siege, and the names of the officers and soldiers who distinguished themselves at that terrific time.

The gate has two ogee-pointed arches, enclosed in rectangular mouldings in the usual Mogul fashion. As one enters the city, inscribed tablets recording incidents of the siege are numerous, and the British authorities have certainly been most careful to preserve the memory of their side of the fight along with the names of their military heroes, and every noteworthy spot in the struggle is commemorated in this way. In addition to such incidental monuments there is the Mutiny Memorial, an important red-sandstone erection (110 feet high) outside the gates, upon a rising ground, and so placed that a complete view can be obtained from its summit of the lines of the siege.

At the fort, which was formerly the Imperial Palace of the Moguls (built in A.D. 1628-58 by Shah Jehan), it is distressing to see the ruthless destruction of superb buildings for which the British have been responsible, and the barbarous way in which hideous barrack structures have been substituted. The fort, or palace, is entered through a noble, deep-red sandstone gate. The Lahore, or, as it is now called, the Victoria Gate, and the fine court, is marred by these ugly modern military barracks for which so much beauty was sacrificed. We were shown two splendid halls, the Diwan-i-am, or public hall of audience, and the Diwan-i-khas, or private-hall of audience. This is of white marble with beautiful inlays of precious stones, with a richly decorated ceiling in colour and gold. A marble pedestal is pointed out as the place whereon the wonderful peacock throne stood. This must indeed have been gorgeous, the seat between two peacocks with spread tails, and these encrusted with sapphires, diamonds, rubies, and emeralds, representing the natural colours of the plumage, a true emblem of oriental magnificence. Over the arches of the arcade in this hall is a Persian inscription in raised and gilt characters, which reads, "If there is a paradise on earth, it is this, it is this, it is this." This costly "paradise," again, was built by the builder of the Taj Mahal, Shah Jehan, who seems to have outshone all the Mogul emperors by the splendour of his buildings. Of course there are no diamonds, or rubies, or emeralds left, and even the small stones used in the decorative floral inlays have in many cases been picked out. It is said that Lord Curzon employed Florentine workmen to replace some of this work at his own expense.

The decoration of the walls and ceilings in the zenana rooms, consisting of painted and gilded arabesques, was very lovely, and the marble Akab Baths exquisite. The river (Jumna) formerly flowed up to the walls of the palace on that side, and from a beautiful minaret we could see the river beyond a belt of green foliage, and get a fine perspective view up and down of the palace wall and buildings.

Near by, on the other side of the court, is the Rung Mahal, which is distinguished by particularly fine pierced screen-work. The vaulted rooms connected with this building were till recently used as officers' mess-rooms, when all their beautiful decoration were obliterated with whitewash.

Opposite to the Akab Baths is the Moti Musjid, called the Pearl Mosque, a most exquisite little building of white marble, a cluster of three domes and many slender pinnacles terminated by lotus flowers. It has many-cusped arches of Saracenic character, and a fine bronze door.

It is sad to think that these lovely buildings are after all only remnants of what were once on this spot when this Imperial Palace was complete in all its splendour. The Burj-i-Shameli, the great marble bath-room; the Metiaz-Mehal, a huge quadrangle of palaces enclosing a garden 300 feet square; the Nobatkhama or music gate, the Golden Mosque, the hareem courts, and fifty other lovely pavilions, fountains, and gardens—think of it! The late W.S. Caine, writing in his "Picturesque India," adds the following passage: "These and other glories of the palace have all been swept away by successive barbarians. Nadir Shah, Ahmed Khan, and the Maratha chiefs were content to strip the buildings of their precious metals and jewelled thrones: to the government of the Empress of India was left the last dregs of vandalism, which, after the Mutiny, pulled down these perfect monuments of Mughal art, to make room for the ugliest brick buildings from Simla to Ceylon."

The Jama Musjid at Delhi is on a splendid scale, a mosque of red sandstone inlaid with white marble. There are four great gateways, approached by long flights of steps, through which the great arcaded square court, in which the mosque stands, is entered. Reputed relics of Buddha are shown to visitors at a shrine at one corner of the court. On the eastern side the mosque faces an open plain from which a large slice of the native city, which once surrounded the mosque, had been cleared by the Government. This gives a clear view of the noble building on this side, but must have been rather distinctive of the character of the place, and one would have thought the mosque, standing so high as it does, would have easily dominated the native houses. In fact, if it had been designed for a site on an open plain, there would have been no necessity to raise it on such a lofty platform. Modern improvers are apt to forget the logic of art.

We went up a side street in the native town on the other side of the mosque to see the Jain temple, which is an interesting and richly decorated small building in the Mogul style of architecture, approached by a doorway in the street and reached by a flight of steps. It is extremely beautiful in detail. In the curious street there were many interesting Mogul doorways. We stopped at a stall to buy some specimens of the glass and lacquered bracelets commonly worn by the native women which only cost a few annas.

The Chandni Chowk (or silver street) is the main business street or bazaar of Delhi. It is very wide, and has a sort of long island down the middle planted with trees. This was said to have been originally an aqueduct. It runs east and west, and we saw a striking effect one evening—the glowing sunset behind the dark masses of the trees, the end of the vista lost in mysterious gloom; twinkling

THE JAMA MUSJID, MOSQUE, DELHI

lights, here and there, about the white awnings of the stalls under the trees; white turbaned figures of natives moving noiselessly up and down, ox-carts and pony tongas, wandering sacred zebus, and all the mixed and varied character of an Indian bazaar form a wonderful and picturesque ensemble.

Individualistic commercial competition is well illustrated in the Chandni Chowk. The traveller is besieged by touts thrusting their cards into his hand, or throwing them into his carriage, or surrounding it with the most importunate solicitations to see their shops.

We visited an ivory carver's workshop in a street leading out of the Chowk. My impression was about this, as in regard to other native handicrafts, that it was now a craft as distinct from an art. We saw the carvers at work, quite a number. It was a species of factory. There were draughtsmen and designers, and miniature painters and inlayers, quite distinct from the carvers. The former draw the patterns on the ivory with a pencil. There were some young boys learning to draw from the craft; one was drawing a bird on a slate. The skill of the ivory-carvers was very wonderful: they could carve a figure inside an open scroll-work and leave it distinct, and there were feats of this kind of which they seemed to be most proud; but these craftsmen seemed to work almost mechanically, no doubt entirely to order, and without any initiative of their own in the way of design. They sat cross-legged on the floor, and more in one room than our factory inspectors would probably approve. The works here were mostly produced for ready sale to the tourist. Elephants and paper knives were—I was going to say, walking hand in hand—all over the shop, and small models of the Taj Mahal ran them close, models of native ox-carts, tongas, and palkis, the native ploughman and his yoke of oxen, and such-like images of familar things of Indian life; elaborate chess-men, and inlaid caskets with little miniatures of the Taj Mahal and the Jama Musjid inserted, in fact all sorts of ivory toys were there, consciously prepared for the Western eye, and too often the Western want of taste. A loquacious Parsee-looking proprietor or manager showed us over this establishment. He had the air of a general director of the works, etc. While not at all pressing, he took care to show all his attractive things, beginning at the most elaborate and costly articles, and skilfully grading downwards, until in price they were within measurable distance of the visitor's purse.

My wife found that native home-spun linen and silks for embroidery were difficult to find in the Chandni Chowk, where there were plenty of European goods.

On January 11th there was a slight frost. The early morning was quite misty, too, but the sun came out later, and there was a strong cold wind from the east in spite of the clear, bright, blue sky and the brilliant sunshine. It suited Delhi far better than the grey sky under which we had seen it the first morning of our visit, and was favourable for our excursion to the Kutab Minar, eleven miles out. Driving through the Delhi and Kashmir Gates again, and along the road past the Jama Musjid, and out again at a farther gate to the south-east, we traversed the region known as Old Delhi, a wonderful tract of ruined cities, shattered buildings, mingled with noble tombs, mosques, and minarets, extending for many miles outside the present city. Domes of tombs were seen on all sides, and broken walls, and the ground was strewn with bricks and stones. Trees (acacias and tamarinds mostly) bordered the road. Our native coachman (a good guide) spoke of No. 8 city, and pointed out its ruined gate, under which we passed. Farther on we took a branch road and stopped before the noble gate of the ancient city of Indrapat with its strong walls and bastions. Leaving our carriage, we passed through the gate and on past a squalid group of wretched huts, where poverty-stricken natives huddled together about their tumble-down dwellings, and where native children were inclined to be rude. Farther along the broken path we reached a spacious octagonal mosque of red sandstone on a marble platform. This was the mosque of Shir Shah (A.D. 1541). The contrast between the dignity of this building and the squalor of the village was striking and saddening.

Resuming our road, we next reached the splendid tomb of Humayun (built by Akbar the Great about 1560 A.D., in memory of his father the Emperor Humayun). An important gateway led into a garden with long tanks and flagged pathways, bordered by formal green hedges, which led up to a spacious platform upon which the noble tomb was built. In the central chamber under the tomb the actual tombstone was screened by pierced marble. There was also a smaller chamber of tombs, each side the central one. The building was of red sandstone, inlaid with white marble with a central dome and four minarets. It seemed to be a prototype of the great Akbar's own tomb we had seen at Sikandra.

Then on again we went, making another short detour from the main road to the cemetery of Nizam-ud-din. Entering through the gateway, we came upon a deep tank, surrounded with buildings. On the flattened dome of one—the Nizam's well-house—sat a group of brown-skinned youths, ready to dive into the water, a dive of about seventy feet, for backsheesh, and the entertainment of the visitor. A passage from this led into a marble court, in the centre of which was the white, marble-domed tomb of the Nizam, brilliantly decorated with arabesques in colour. It reminded one of the shrine of the Kwaja in the Dargarh at Ajmir. There were also other tombs in the court, one to the poet Khusru, whose songs are said to be still popular in India. An interesting one is that of Jahanara Begum, daughter of the Emperor Shah Jehan, on which is an inscription to the effect that she begs that nothing but grass may cover her. Certainly her wishes are fulfilled, as the grass grows freely in the marble-sided tomb which has no cover. Up some steps was the modern tomb of Mirza Jahangir, but a beautiful marble one.

The carving in marble and ornaments of all these tombs were exceedingly delicate and beautiful, and would compare well with the work on the Taj Mahal.

The visitor on leaving is embarrassed by the

number of claimants of fees. There seemed to be a different custode for every tomb in the place, and the crowd of hangers-on, hungry for backsheesh, rather spoils the pleasure which the sight of so much beautiful work gives.

Returning to the road again and continuing our drive, it was not long before we descried the great Kutab Minar rising up above the trees in front of us. We had indeed caught a glimpse of it miles away, when the tower was almost lost in the haze. There is a good little bungalow close by where the traveller can get tiffin, or put up for the night if so minded.

The Minar, tapering upwards to an astonishing height (238 feet), piercing the clear blue sky, is of red sandstone with a white marble top story. There are five stories, and the summit was formerly crowned by a small cupola and open arcade, which was destroyed by a storm, and a model of it has been placed near by. Successive bands of small carving are carried across the deep flutings, both semicircular and rectangular alternately on the lower storey, semicircular in the second, rectangular in the third, a plain cylinder forming the fourth, while the fifth and last is partly fluted and partly plain. These bands are composed of texts from the Koran, the Arabic characters having a rich ornamental effect, the carving being wonderfully sharp and unimpaired, although it dates from the twelfth and the latter part of the thirteenth century (A.D. 1210-20), having been built as a tower of Victory, commenced by Kutab-ud-din, and completed by his successor, Altamsh.

The tower was built in the centre of the old Hindu fortress of Lalkot (A.D. 1060). At its foot are various ruins, the most extensive being those of a fine Mohammedan mosque, constructed out of the materials of, and incorporated with an ancient Hindu temple, the original columns of the latter remaining to form the colonnade of the court.

The images of the Hindu gods have been mostly defaced when they occurred in the carving.

There is a fine Mogul arch of red sandstone, similar in treatment and style to "the mosque of two and a half days" at Ajmir. In front of this, in the centre of the court, stands a remarkable pillar of solid wrought iron, supposed to date from A.D. 300 to 400. It is dedicated to Vishnu, and there are lines in Sanscrit inscribed around it. The wonder is that such a massive thing in iron could have been forged at that early period.

Returning to Delhi by a different road we passed another important-looking tomb, also near the outskirts of the present city, the ruins of the Observatories built by different rajahs in the eighteenth century, which impress one as weighty evidences of the philosophical knowledge and culture of these native princes. A moon observatory was pointed out to us, and a vast circular building. The groups of ruined buildings hereabout recalled to us the Roman Campagna and its fragments.

Our coachman (who was perhaps more careful as a guide than as a Jehu) collided rather violently with a tonga just outside the city, and the consequences might have been serious, but the wheels were the chief sufferers, and the tonga must have got the worst of the jolt, one of the native passengers being thrown out. No bones were broken, and the incident did not seem to be

DELHI DRIVING. WANTED—A RULE OF THE ROAD

regarded as at all an unusual occurrence. There seems no rule of the road in India, and so risks are constantly run. In the crowded streets the drivers rely on the power of their lungs to shout out warnings of their approach, and it is a marvel people escape being run over, and that collisions are not more frequent and worse than they are.

At the hotel, where the custom of small, separate,

circular dining-tables obtained, we happened to meet a very agreeable Anglo-American family from Ceylon, who were travelling in India, and were returning to their home at Colombo, before visiting Japan and Europe. We discovered we had several friends in common, and promised to visit them when we came to Ceylon.

I got a coloured drawing of the Jama Musjid from the plain before mentioned, where a few trees afforded a little shade, the sun being very strong, although a cool wind was still blowing from the east. The light was particularly clear and the shadows sharp, so that the architecture looked remarkably distinct, the effect being almost hard.

We had a stroll in the park-like grounds near the Club. There was an old and much overgrown Mogul archway here, which had been considerably battered in the siege. There were fine cypresses and other trees, and among them little flights of green parroquets flew with their shrill scream—their flight and their notes reminding one of our swifts. Toucans were also to be seen, and of course the palm squirrels. We watched a whole colony of them sleeping in the hollow of a fine old banyan tree.

CHAPTER X

AMRITZAR AND LAHORE

WE left Delhi by a night train—the Punjab Mail—for Amritzar, but we had a long wait at the station, as the train was two hours late. The station was thronged with natives bound for some religious festival connected with the approaching eclipse of the sun. There was a seething mass of dark humanity at the entrance, through which we had almost to fight our way to the platform.

Our route was by way of Umballa, which we reached in the early morning. The country was wrapped in a thick white mist before the sun rose, when it gradually cleared. Beyond Umballa the country was very flat, the dry lands varied with green crops and yellow with charlock, as before, and dotted with acacia trees. Occasionally we crossed wide rivers, or river beds, and the usual flocks of white cranes and brown kites were seen. Jullumpore was another junction where our train stopped. It looked an interesting place from the railway, a walled town with towers and ancient mosques. After leaving Pillour (the refreshment station) a very broad river was crossed, and on the wide sands of the dry part of its bed, almost like a desert, we saw a train of thirty camels moving slowly in single file.

We did not reach Amritzar until about 1 P.M., more than three hours after time! On emerging from the station, despite our bearer, we were nearly torn to pieces by hotel touts.

The Alexandra hotel had been named to us and

SHE WON'T BE HAPPY TILL SHE GETS EVERYTHING PACKED UP

we asked for its representative, but it appeared there was no such hotel at Amritzar. Each rival tout clamoured for our custom, declaring that the hotel he represented was the true and only successor to the mythical Alexandra.* One went so far as to

* We learned afterwards that it was the custom to change the names of hotels every six months or so.

say he had received a post-card from us, but when asked to produce it only showed a letter from some one else! Finally we got into a carriage,

DEMON HOTEL TOUTS AT AMRITZAR FIGHTING FOR THEIR PREY

which was immediately stormed by the irrepressible touts, one seating himself on the box, one on the step each side, and I don't know how many hanging on behind. Not liking the look of the first hotel they took us to, we tried a second and decided to put up there, and so gradually shook off the touts. There was more of an Eastern character about our quarters here than we had hitherto experienced. The hotel was quite an Oriental serai in an Eastern garden, our rooms being in a sort of Indian villa, opening on to a terrace with steps down into the garden, with its narrow straight paths between fruit trees, and our room was rather like a small temple or chapel with recessed walls and ogee arched doorways, a raftered ceiling, and clerestory windows. Built for coolness, no doubt, we now found it positively cold in the mornings and evenings, and although there was a fireplace the lighting of a wood fire made matters worse, for we were nearly smoked out.

There were several English or Anglo-English at table preserving their characteristic frigidity in the presence of strangers. A gentleman from Manchester was the only one who showed a friendly disposition and who had any conversation.

Driving through the city we had recourse to smelling-bottles, as owing to the open drains each side the streets the odours which saluted our nostrils were rather trying. I had noticed· these open gulleys at Delhi and in the native quarters in other towns. They run close in front of the houses and open shops of the bazaars, and are crossed by slabs of stone placed across them at intervals to give access to the houses, and as all sorts of refuse finds its way into them it is not surprising they should be offensive sometimes, though it had not been nearly so noticeable elsewhere. Amritzar is said to have the benefit of the advice of an English sanitary engineer.

The street did not strike us as so varied and

interesting as other cities we had seen, and the house fronts seemed plainer and more modern, as a rule, though the streets were narrow enough.

From a sort of terrace we got our first view of the Golden Temple, which is built in the centre of

THROUGH AMRITZAR—SIT TIGHT AND HOLD A SMELLING BOTTLE!

the large tank or lake in the centre of the city. A broad paved causeway connects with the paved walk along two sides of the lake. After the magnificent and beautifully proportioned Mogul architecture of Agra and Delhi, the Golden Temple, built at the beginning of the nineteenth century is rather disappointing, despite its gilded domes, the building looking rather squat, though the gold reflected in the rippling water has a charming effect. The gilded dome of the Atal tower also shows over the buildings behind the temple seen from the terrace. Leaving our carriage at this spot we were surrounded and eyed by a curious crowd. Rival guides apparently contended for us, and there was a sudden quarrel, ending in a free fight, between two of them, the end of which we did not remain to see. The temple and its precincts is held most sacred by the Sikhs, Amritzar being their religious centre, the place is most jealously watched. It seemed impossible to get away from the crowd, who appeared to be none too friendly to strangers, and sketching was out of the question without a bodyguard.

We had a very courteous and kind reception from Dr Dinghra, three of whose sons we had known in London. One son and his wife were staying with him, and we spent a pleasant hour under his hospitable roof, and he presented us with handsome saddle bags, made of the local carpet, on leaving. He also introduced us to one of the leading citizens, a magistrate, who had an extensive pile carpet manufactory, and he showed us over the works. These were long sheds, having round arched arcades opening on to a court, and in these were a series of high-warp hand-looms with rows of shuttles filled with the different coloured wools hanging from the top. The weavers sat, or rather squatted, in a row on the ground in front of the warp and worked in the pattern. They were young boys and youths trained to the work early. They used a small curved knife like a small sickle to shear off the ends of their threads and press them home when a particular bit of coloured pattern was finished. Little oblong labels written in Arabic were placed on the warp in front of each weaver, which gave the written directions for the colours to be used in the work. No individual judgment or choice appeared to be exercised by the weavers.

There was a design room also open to the court under an arcade, here some quite aged natives were preparing designs, sketching them out in pencil or charcoal on squared paper, quite in the European method, and in some cases working from photographs of special carpets.

I learned from the manager that the working hours in this factory were from 8 A.M. till dark. The boy weavers only got one and a half annas a day! We finally were shown the finished product —a whole series of large handsome carpets being rolled out for us to see. One of these, of a Persian kind of design, would be priced at 200 rupees, the manager said. Before leaving we were requested to write our names, and any remarks on our visit, in a visitor's book, where the list had been headed by the Prince and Princess of Wales, who visited these works on their tour in India in 1905.

In the forenoon of January 14th we saw the eclipse of the sun from our terrace. It rather took us by surprise—the light quickly becoming curiously pale like moonlight and the air unusually chilly. We could see the sun turned into a crescent quite distinctly, and pass through various phases like a moon, till it gradually regained its normal shape and power shortly after noon.

As we sat on the terrace a native pedlar

approached with two portentous bundles. He salaamed, and proceeded to unload his wares in front of us. His stock, however, consisted entirely of

AN INDIAN AUTOLYCUS

European goods—small wares such as tapes and buttons, studs, soaps and perfumes, patent medicines, and such articles as are supposed to meet the wants of travellers. This Indian Autolycus addressed us as "Father" and "Mother," and like the "Mad Hatter" commenced his speeches by saying "me very poor man," following this announcement by urgent appeals to us to buy, after each purchase, beginning all over again afresh. Probably he felt he had to make the most of his English, as well as of his stock and his opportunities.

After another look at the Golden Temple, which it was impossible to approach without a crowd and without clumsy canvas shoes over our own, we made our way round to the Atal tower. Here, again, before entering the anything but clean marble court shoes had to be put off. It is an octagonal shrine, or tomb, having curious beaten metal plates, gilded figure designs in repoussé over the doors, but the decorative art here was much inferior in design and detail to what we had seen further south.

We then drove to the public gardens in which stands the pavilion of Ranji Singh. The gardens are full of beautiful palms and trees of many different kinds, including fine cypresses and splendid clumps of bamboos. The roads around Amritzar are lined with trees, and one sees enormous banyans spreading their great branches and masses of dark green foliage and casting deep shadows on the long avenues. Large plantations and fruit gardens, too, surround the city, so that it has a very attractive look although on a dead level.

Oranges of a large rough-skinned kind are grown here. They are deep-coloured, and more like lemons in shape. There was also a very small circular orange about the size of a large cherry in the hotel garden, where roses, pansies, and violets were blooming freely. The native gardener was generally to the fore in offering us small posies or buttonholes whenever he had an opportunity and for a consideration.

We left Amritzar for Lahore on January the 15th, having another long wait for the Punjab mail, this time three hours behind time. However, about noon another train came up and we were advised by the stationmaster to go on by that in preference to waiting longer for the mail. This train, he said, would take us to Lahore more quickly than the quick train, which sounds like a contradiction in terms. It is only about an hour's journey.

The country between Amritzar and Lahore is, again, flat and has no striking features. Fields under irrigation green with young crops of corn, often smothered in charlock, alternated with dry fields or the standing canes of ripe crops, and stubbles of some newly reaped. The wells were plentiful. Some of the irrigation wells in this district are of a different pattern and mechanism to the simple draw-well seen generally. A pair of oxen turn a horizontal heavy wooden wheel which has slots at regular intervals around the outside of its rim. These slots catch the projecting spokes or straight cogs of another wheel, also horizontally placed and smaller in size, and this in turn by means of the cogs moves a large water wheel arranged in a vertical position, the projecting cogs catching the spokes of this wheel, which has a series of leather buckets or water pots attached to its broad rim, on the same principle as we see in dredging machines. As the wheel turns the buckets are dipped one after the other into the well, and as they rise again full empty their contents into a trough immediately in front of the wheel, which communicates with another trough connected with the irrigating trenches, which are thus supplied with water.

The station at Lahore was comparatively quiet and was a pleasing contrast to the turbulent crowd at Amritzar. The Charing Cross hotel received us, but anything less suggestive of the associations its name recalled it would be difficult to imagine. It was of the usual extended bungalow type, with long arcades in front of ranges of ground floor rooms, spacious and lofty and reminding rather of the vast rooms one sees on the stage with raftered ceilings and whitewashed walls. The lower wall of our sitting-room, however, was hung with very interesting Indian hand-painted cotton hangings, which gave it rather a distinguished appearance. There was a bedroom, something between a prison and a chapel, and dressing and the usual bath rooms, with zinc tubs, opening out beyond. There were large sitting and dining rooms, the latter an enormous one, like the nave of a church, lighted by a clerestory only, and cold enough, where people dined rather frigidly, each group at a safe distance at separate little round tables. We were glad of a log-fire in the evenings, though the sun was powerful enough during the day. "The Charing Cross post office" was close by, which had one pigeon hole, and where the stamps were sold outside under the verandah, by a native squatting on the ground.

A fine broad avenue through the English quarter is called "The Mall," and here the principal government buildings are situated, the Law courts and the Museum, and the principal stores and bungalows. This British residential and business quarter is quite distinct and lies quite clear outside the walls of the native city of Lahore. It is laid out in broad drives with tan rides at the side,

ENJOYING A LOG FIRE AT LAHORE

and bordered with trees. Bungalows and shops and stores in the shape of bungalows standing detached in gardens are arranged pleasantly from the modern residential point of view, and forms quite a "garden city," only marred by the atrocious way in which the traders announce their names and business in staring white block-letters on black boards. One piano warehouse, I noticed, had even a sky sign. Even the private residences are often disfigured in the same way by black boards with the name of the occupier in the ugliest block-letters.

The gardens and hedges, often of roses trained on trellises of bamboo, are kept very trim up and down the Mall.

Smart English ladies and officers ride or drive about in their dog-carts with native tigers behind. We met a very imposing and original turn out—a fine pair of brown camels, well matched, were harnessed to a sort of barouche, each ridden, postilion-wise, by native servants in scarlet, one in the same colour behind the carriage, which contained two English ladies. This was probably the Lieutenant-Governor's carriage. Bicycles were much in use both by Europeans' (men and women) and natives—the turban and loose pyjama-like clothes of the latter looking strange on the machine. The natives, however, everywhere in the towns where the Europeans' influence comes in seem to take to machines. The sewing machine is constantly seen in the bazaars, always, however, worked by a man. A certain firm's poster of the eternal woman enclosed in a hideous S (like a modern Eve and the industrial serpent) looks particularly incongruous and out of place in India, where there seems to be no women working at crafts. The men do the washing too, the Dhobee in white with his bundle of linen being a frequent and characteristic figure.

No greater contrast could be imagined than that between the English quarter and the native city lying within its old walls and great gates, with its narrow picturesque streets and—stinks! Open drains as at Amritzar run along each side of the streets, close in front of the bazaar, where the people sit. The fronts of the houses above the open shops are mostly of wood of a dark rich tone, corbelled arcaded balconies and windows jutting out over the street at all sorts of angles, rich with delicate and varied carvings, as if the builders had vied with each other which should make the most interesting front. There are charming little covered verandahs and balconies with slender columns and ogee arches, and pierced screen-work painted here and there, but mostly the deep dusky brown tone of the natural wood, dark with age, which forms an effective background to the vivid colours and glitter of costumes and draperies of the bazaars. The newly dyed long strips of cotton or muslin in orange or pink, green or lemon yellow which are hung out to dry, wave like long banners over the busy life of the narrow streets, where the turbaned and many coloured, swarthy faced crowd, jostle along, or stand in chattering groups about the shops, buying and selling. The types, too, are very varied—the Hindu, the Mohammedan, the Afghan, the country folk; the Mohammedan woman in trousers, the Hindu woman in her graceful Sari, with her glittering silver anklets, and bracelets, toe-rings and nose-rings; dark eyes and shining whites momentarily seen, and gleaming teeth, the mysterious looking figures covered from head to foot in flowing white drapery, pleated into a close fitting cap, with little perforations for the eyes, in front, the effect of the whole being ghostly, or even ghoulish. The white mystery being only betrayed by a brown foot beneath and the gleam of a silver anklet which tells one it is only the disguise of a Mohammedan woman.

"THE WOMAN IN WHITE" AT LAHORE (SUGGESTION FOR A DISGUISE PARTY)

Here again it was rather disappointing to see the native bazaars full of European goods, and a trivial cheap kind at that. European commerce has evidently got its foot in. Blue enamelled basins and cups, tin ware, tapes and buttons, braces, socks and ugly woollen scarfs in aniline colours are seen everywhere. It is true that one occasionally may see a nàtive handicraftsman at work, such as the man who prints the ornamental borders on the edges of the muslin veils of the women, and picks them out in silver leaf, silver or orange being a favourite arrangement. The metal-worker is also frequent, though he often only makes zinc stoves. The food shops are the most numerous, set out with piles of curious yellow cakes and sweets of all sorts and sizes, the cooking stove being often in front of the shop, made of clay or mud with a tiny hole in which they produce hot little fires.

Through the bazaars our carriage worked its way as through a labyrinth. The mixed throng of buyers and sellers, beggars and brown babies, and cheeky little street Arabs, who are inclined to be rude to the stranger generally, tongas, buffaloes, herds of goats, stray zebu bulls, and fat-tailed sheep.

These latter we first saw at Delhi. They are originally from Tibet. The enormous development of the tail, or fleece of the tail, has a very extraordinary effect, as if the animal carried a bag of wool behind it, both broad and long and nearly touching the ground. Occasionally we saw one of these animals (rams) dyed with orange colour, and marked with curious patterns all over its fleece.

Passing through the bazaars we arrived at a large open space, and soon reached the (Roshanai) gate of the Fort on the other side of it. There the English sentry, after saying an order was necessary, called an orderly to take us round. Just inside the gate we got a view of the old wall of the palace decorated by tiles, the colours being similar to those used at Gwalior, at the Man-Mandir palace, principally turquoise, green, and lemon yellow, the tile-work being arranged in bands or friezes of elephants and birds in profile, let into the red sandstone.

The very stolid British "Tommy" in khaki conducted us, in slow marching order and in solemn silence, up the long sloping road to the square of the Fort where he pointed out, without emotion, a colonnaded Hall of audience, and then took us through a gateway into the rather spacious court of the old palace of Akbar, who also built the Fort. On one side of the court was an interesting armoury of Sikh weapons, beginning with suits of fine chain mail and Persian-looking steel topis, damasceened and bossed circular targes up to flint-locks, and match-locks, and blunderbusses.

There was quite a mediæval-looking heavy steel mace, and many sabres, and sword sticks, some made with crutch handles terminating in horses' heads. There were also a number of steel cuirasses. I believe this armoury was arranged by Mr Kipling, the father of Mr Rudyard Kipling, who was head of the art school of Lahore for many years, and to whom is due the extremely interesting museum.

There were relics of elaborate decoration on the walls and vaults of what remained of the palace, and some of the glass (convex-mirror-mosaic) work united with gesso-relief ornament, which we saw at Udaipur, Amber, Delhi, and other places: but the British occupation had tried its best, by introducing hideous chunks of barrack buildings, to take the romance and beauty out of the place.

Close to the Fort outside its gate is the Samadh, or burning-place of Ranjit Singh. A carved lotus flower, surrounded by eleven smaller ones, on a raised platform inside the pavilion-like building, mark the place where his body was burned with eleven ladies of his Zenana. Not far off rises the dome of the Jama Musjid and its noble minarets of red sandstone.

There is a fine park-like country beyond the walls on this side of the city with groups of old trees. The minarets and domes of Lahore have a striking effect seen from outside the gate. We returned through the bazaars a different way, passing the golden domed mosque and also the Wazar Khan mosque, the latter a very fine one fronting a small square in the middle of the city, and having two large minarets faced with enamelled tiles in blue and green and other colours, cobalt predominating. The spandrils of the main entrance, and in fact the whole of the front, being decorated with tiles in large arabesques and borderings, a large Arabic text in blue written boldly over the arch, and panels down each flank of smaller scale work. It was the first tiled mosque we had seen, and quite characteristic of the art of a district which culminates in the renowned tombs at Multan.

At the English club house on the Mall, the pipers of a Highland regiment were playing on the lawn in front. The club had well laid out and ample lawn tennis courts, large blue durries being hung at each end of the courts to stop the balls, and the players had native caddies to pick them up. There were zoological gardens near by where we saw nylghaus and antelopes and birds of various sorts.

A Victoria memorial on a large scale was in progress at a place where branching roads met. The work of the British sculptor in India cannot be said to be much more exhilarating than the work of the British architect, as a rule, to judge from the specimens we saw, chiefly of statues of the late Queen Victoria.

The courts of Justice at Lahore are more successful than most of the modern examples in India, perhaps because designed in what might be called the local style—the Mogul. Near by in a little garden enclosed by clipped hedges was a bronze statue of Lord Laurence offering the choice of government by pen or sword to the passer by. It had some dramatic expression, though the choice of a momentary attitude in a portrait statue is perhaps open to criticism.

We visited the museum, where Mr Percy Brown has succeeded Mr Kipling as director. Here is a most interesting collection of typical native textiles, including the raised wax designs gilded, silvered, and lacquered on grounds of different coloured cloths, an art which is still practised in the district with success, traditional designs of flowers and birds being repeated in a very skilful and effective way, and applied to the adornment of portières, covers, etc. There were also good collections of native jewellery and enamels. Champlévé enamel, such as is done at Lucknow, was illustrated by specimens in different stages from the commencement to the finish, side by side with cloissoné (Japanese) illustrated in the same complete way, as well as complete models showing native industries and handicrafts in operation; interesting old Hindu herbals and manuscripts on vellum with characteristic miniatures; drawings of local palaces and gardens in plan, elevation and bird's-eye perspective.

There was a very notable collection of Greco-Buddhist sculptures, which were extremely interesting and unusual.

Very little wood-carving, curiously enough, except modern examples in screens and furniture, the work of the Art School, exhibited in a separate room. The city of Lahore being so rich in carved wood-work it was less necessary to have it in the museum, and, of course, much better to see it *in situ*. The modern way of selling the spoils of old buildings to private collections or to museums is carried on in Europe to an alarming extent, so that one begins to fear, in view of the rapid destruction of ancient houses now going on, whether there will soon be left any genuine bits of antiquity in this commercial world. It is better of course that relics of ancient art should find a haven in a public museum than that it should perish altogether, but any destruction or removal for the express purpose of transportation to a museum should be deprecated.

On the whole the Lahore museum was a well-chosen and arranged museum, judiciously limited to Indian art, and it was interesting to see the groups of natives—men, women, and children—

apparently scanning the different objects with the greatest interest and with much animated conversation among themselves. One afternoon we drove to the Waza Khan Mosque, and I made the sketch reproduced here of the entrance to the mosque from the carriage. The crowd was curious, but not nearly so troublesome as elsewhere, and our conductor, or running footman, kept them off pretty well. The square had large pools of mud in it here and there after recent rains. Zebus were straying about, or lying down. Fruit and good stalls occupied other parts of the ground, and ox-carts deposited loads of wood. Men sat in groups in the porch of the mosque, or on the steps, from which boys flew their little diamond-shaped paper kites. The mysterious-looking white figures of the Mohammedan women wandered about like substantial ghosts. We saw a pretty little gazelle at one of the stalls, perfectly tame, and a great pet of the native who owned it.

The Cashmere travelling merchants, who display their tempting wares at all the hotels, spread out their stuffs in profusion—Bokhara embroideries, Persian covers, kincobs, turbans, and portières of black, red, or green grounds, effectively decorated with designs in the raised wax, such as we saw in the museum—and used all their persuasive arts to effect sales.

We did not stay long enough in Lahore to see much of the Society there, but before leaving we had a visit from the Princess Duleep Singh and her sister, who, hearing from friends at Amritzar that we were there, came to see us at the hotel.

The princess was dressed as a Parsee lady in beautiful classical draperies, white with embroidered borders, and she drove herself in a dog-cart, but the sister was in European dress. The princess

THE MERCHANTS OF KASHMIR

recalled the circumstance of my having made a little sketch in her brother the prince's cottage on the Norfolk coast, which had been designed for him by Mr Detmar Blow, which we visited when staying in the neighbourhood.

We left Lahore the mid-day Lucknow Mail, after a long wait, the platform covered with picturesque groups of squatting natives. We

LAHORE—THE MOSQUE OF WAZA KHAN

eventually shared a compartment, as far as Umballa, with an English official, his German wife and a little girl. As far as Umballa on this line, coming north, we had already journeyed. The chief incident after leaving Lahore was the catching fire of one of the boxes of one of the carriages of our train, which caused the passengers hastily to leave it, and crowd into other parts of the train, when it was stopped and the burning carriage taken off at a small station just before Amritzar.

At Umballa, the dining station, which we reached when it was dark, some said we had to change, others said not. This was puzzling. One official with more authority than the others said emphatically "no," at last. So, having just time, we scurried across the bridge to the refreshment room with light hearts and sharp appetites, snatched a hasty meal and hurried back to find Moonsawmy, who acted as courier and took charge of the tickets, in some difficulty with the officials about the tickets. One official (the stationmaster) came up, and then said we ought to have changed into the train which was just at that moment steaming out of the station, excusing his mistake by saying that he had not till then seen our tickets, fussily ordering a humble Hindu clerk to take the numbers.

After this we got into our compartment again and settled ourselves for a sleep, as we were not due at Lucknow until next morning. During the night we were constantly disturbed by people opening the carriage door and peering in—no doubt in search of lower berths, which we occupied. At one place a Eurasian got in with a quantity of baggage, and got out again only a few stations off. On leaving, perceiving he had disturbed us he said he was "sorry for the trouble,"

At Barielly another man (English) got in with his traps and rugs and settled himself to sleep on the middle berth—which in some carriages economises space between the two side ones—though he was at first a little taken aback at seeing that one of us was a lady. However, he turned out to be a very agreeable companion afterwards, and we got quite friendly as the train the next morning approached Lucknow, we having previously decided not to stop at Cawnpore.

CHAPTER XI

LUCKNOW

ARRIVING at Lucknow in due course we parted with our fellow traveller, who was met by the military chaplain, and we did not see him again. The chaplain kindly gave us some information, and said that the hotel we were bound for was reputed to be "the best in India." This was good hearing, and we found it quite borne out by our experience of Wurtzler's, where we presently found ourselves in comfortable rooms, bungalow-like, opening on to a verandah. The hotel had formerly been a palace, and was rather a handsome building in its way, with a round-arched arcaded front, long and low, with a pleasant enclosure of trees and flower garden.

There was "a little rift within the lute," however, which rather marred the first moments of our arrival at Lucknow, my wife having unfortunately got a little bit of grit in her eye from the engine while in the train. There was nothing for it but to drive to the hospital the first thing after breakfast. Luckily we caught the chief surgeon (Col. Anderson) just as he was attending to some native cases in waiting. He at once took us to the "operating room," which sounded rather fearsome, and was indeed a severe place with a polished marble floor, a case of surgical instruments and an operating table being the only furniture visible. The poor eye-patient had to extend herself on the

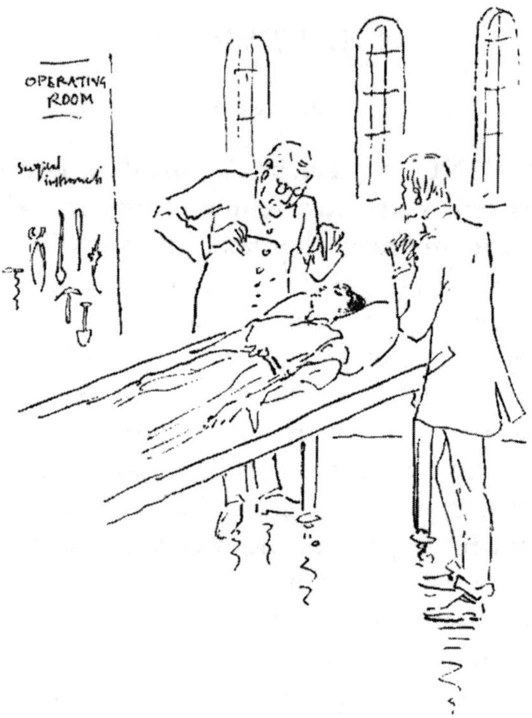

IN HOSPITAL, LUCKNOW. THE OPERATING TABLE (PATIENT HAD A BIT OF GRIT IN HER EYE AFTER A TRAIN JOURNEY)—SIXTEEN RUPEES WERE EXTRACTED!

table, while the Colonel very deftly found and quickly removed a tiny black speck which had caused all the trouble—working up right under the upper lid of the eye. He put some cocaine into the eye first of all, and afterwards applied a little lint and lotion. The relief must have been worth anything—it might have been described as a lesser Relief of Lucknow!

The next example of human skill or sleight of hand we witnessed was in the juggling, not the surgical, profession. It was a native conjurer who, under the arcade of the hotel, showed us the famous mango tree trick. As additional attractions, or a

JUGGLERS AT LUCKNOW—THE MANGO TREE TRICK

sort of side-show, he had a large cobra in a round box, which, when the lid was off, reared its head all alive and hissing, and ready for a performance with a well-to-do mongoose, which was held in readiness by a cord tied tightly round its neck, which is apparently the only way in which to secure a mongoose.

The man commenced his performance by placing a monkey's skull on the pavement, and sticking a little china doll up in front of it. Then he produced a very dry-looking mango seed about the size of a small potato, and this he planted carefully in an ordinary earthen flower-pot, covering the seed with soil, and then watering it, muttering some unknown words over it. He then put it under a cloth raised tentwise by a stick, to let it grow, as he said, while he went on with a number of small but very skilful conjuring tricks with cards, coins, marbles, ring and handkerchief, etc., any of which he offered to teach. Presently he lifted the cloth and showed the mango tree sending up a shoot of fresh green, and apparently growing vigorously. Then he covered it up again and performed some more tricks, after which he again uncovered the mango, which now showed a stem and bunch of leaves at the top like a miniature tree. Finally, after another interval of a few minutes juggling and conjuring, he lifted the cloth again, and, holding the pot in one hand, he pulled up the little mango tree with the other, showing it had stem, roots, and all. The man had an assistant, but he only played a very subordinate part, handing the conjurer the various things he wanted from time to time, holding the mongoose, but not performing in any way. These wonders were to be seen for the fee of three rupees. The conjurer was very proud of his "chits" which he showed, and among the signatures were those of "Castlereagh" and "Wenlock"; and he asked for a written testimonial in his book.

At Lucknow we had an introduction to the Chief Commissioner, Mr Ross Scott, who received us very cordially at his charming house, and offered to do anything for us. Among other kindnesses he sent my wife (whose health had suffered from the climate everywhere in India) a supply of excellent milk from his own cows during her stay, which proved of immense benefit. At his house we met Mrs Dowden and her daughter, who kindly undertook to show us over the ruins of the Residency which were quite close by. The building stands, or what remains of it after the bombardment it sustained during the terrible days of "the Mutiny," amid pleasant lawns and fine trees, and creepers cover the ruins. In one of the rooms is a good model of the Residency as it was in 1857 in the midst of the native city on a rising ground, but thickly surrounded by the houses and mosques, from which guns and mortars were trained on to it. These were shown planted on flat roofs or in courtyards, wherever there was vantage ground. Nothing but a few shapeless ruins remain hereabouts now of the old native city, which has since been curtailed and cut in two by a broad road for the rapid movement of troops. However savage and cruel the sepoys may have been, the British reprisals were certainly severe. They seemed to have practically "wiped out" old Lucknow afterwards. We were shown a building—the Sikander Bagh—a high-walled enclosure, once a fair rose-garden, which was taken by Colin Campbell, and where 2000 rebels were bayoneted without mercy by the British troops. A young English officer, speaking professionally, perhaps, we met at a friend's house, said that Sikander Bagh gave him more satisfaction than any other memorial of the mutiny. He positively "gloated over it," and intended to go there again and "gloat." It is said even that British soldiers bayoneted even the sick and wounded Hindu soldiers in the hospitals who begged to be shot instead!

The whole place is overshadowed by memories of that awful period. Nothing can impair the courage and endurance of the heroic defenders of the Residency; but it is now, I believe, generally admitted that the outbreak was not without its causes, and that the government of the day did not act judiciously, to say the least. It is commonly called "The Mutiny," but it was really an insurrection, which must from various causes have been smouldering for some time before it burst into flame. The "greased cartridges" were only the last straw. There seems to have been much discontent. Many sepoys, too, had been disbanded. The British annexation, the deposition and deportation of the reigning King of Oudh and the confiscation of his revenues, must all be considered as provocative causes; and it is a question whether at any time British rule has made itself loved in India, or the British residents have ever really understood the Indian people. Native feeling must have been generally ignored.

It was a formidable revolt, accompanied, no doubt, by explosions of race hatred and by terrible cruelties, but there was savagery on both sides—a desperate attempt to regain possession of their own country and its government on the part of the princes and people.

The question remains, with all the official

solicitude of the British government for the welfare of the natives, all the railways, engineering, and irrigation works, are they really better off than they were under native rule?

Are they not, though under British administration, more heavily taxed than they were under the native kings? Mr William Digby, C.I.E., who had long personal and official experience in India, brings a formidable array of facts and statistics (from official sources, too), in his "Prosperous British India," in support of the view that they *are*, and, moreover, that the ryot—the tiller of the soil—is gradually becoming poorer under our rule.

To a passing observer, the Hindus—nay, the people of India, either Hindus or Mohammedans—can never be Europeanised. There is a great gulf between the East and the West. After all these years of British occupation and administration, the two races live entirely apart and separate. In religion, manners, and customs, and sentiment, they are fundamentally different, opposed, one might say.

The British remain a transitory garrison of military and civil administrative aliens, in the midst of vast populations, rooted in the traditions, religious beliefs and observances of untold centuries, during which they have carried on the same mode of life, and who seem neither to seek or to desire change.

The mere struggle to live must occupy the energies of the vast majority, but among the more educated and leisured classes of natives there is a growing feeling of what we should call nationalism in Europe, though it may be more strictly racial than national. It is difficult, however, to see how anything like a universal movement over the whole peninsula could arise, considering the differences of caste, race and religion, or the wide differences which separate Hindus and Mohammedans. Some, however, rather think that political change may be forced by bankruptcy, considering the poverty of the people and the limits of taxation being reached.

We were shown, at the Residency, the room where Sir Henry Laurence was struck with the shell, the holes its explosion made in the wall, his grave also, and many other memorials which have a profound interest for the English visitors. Old rust-eaten, muzzle-loading muskets, sabres, and shot and shell, with which the Residency was peppered, were collected in a group in one of the rooms, and the place, as far as possible, has been made an historical museum of the period of the siege.

Our friends introduced us at the Chatter Manzel, formerly a palace of the kings of Oudh, but now used as an English club. The rooms were of spacious and good proportions—long in comparison with their width. Proportion, in fact, is the principal notable quality of the local architecture at Lucknow, the details being comparatively commonplace after the beautiful inventive detail and decoration of the Mogul architects at Delhi and Agra, the ornamentation being mostly mere repetitions. After the marble inlay of the Taj Mahal and the Diwan-ud-Daulat, and Sikandra, or the rich arabesques of the Zenana rooms at Amber, the white and yellow wash and the rather coarse plaster work of the palaces and pavilions of Lucknow look, comparatively speaking, cheap. The stuccoed domes of the mosques miss the splendour of the gold and ivory-like marble seen elsewhere. Even the Jama Musjid, fine in scale as it is, lacks the charm of colour. There was a smaller mosque near the old stone bridge, however, which stood out against the deep-blue sky in dazzling whiteness, but this only showed how beautiful plain whitewash appears illuminated by the Indian sun—pearly with delicate reflections and warm shadows.

The Iambara had a beautifully-proportioned court, with steps up to the pavilion, the symmetry of the spacing being rather pleasantly broken by the mosque on one side being placed at a different angle in order to point to the direction of Mecca, as all Mohammedan mosques must do.

Inside the pavilion, under canopies of heavy embroidery in gold and silver, supported by chased silver poles, were the tombs of one of the kings and his zenana. On the walls were mirrors which reminded us of our English empire-period framed mantle-glasses. Some of these had curious tempera paintings inserted in their frames of native birds and trees, and there were other Indian paintings, one showing General or Captain Martin—the French adventurer who founded the Martinière at Lucknow in the early nineteenth century—in a blue coat and gold lace and white nankeen trousers, like a naval officer of that period, conferring with the King of Oudh and his court. An image of a winged horse (a Buddhist symbol) strikingly resembled the Assyrian type of winged man-headed creatures, the treatment being remarkably similar. The crowned head, with long, black, curled locks, and formal, rather small, wings, with each feather expressed. There was an umbrella attached, which moved to and fro over the head of the figure by clock-work.

We were interested to see in the Daulat Khan—a sort of gallery up a steep flight of steps—a series of full-length portraits of the kings of Oudh in their robes, painted by English artists. Most of these were signed by my friend T. Erat Harrison, 1882-4, and I recalled the fact of having seen him at work on one of them about that time.

An English lady, Mrs Dowden (wife of Colonel Dowden), was kind enough to conduct us through Lucknow and its wonders, and she proved an excellent cicerone, and waved off all unnecessary attentions from caretakers and their hangers-on with the decisive air of a resident.

We passed a hideous clock tower—one of many in India—put up by some modern architect (as a Jubilee memorial, I think). It is astonishing what monstrosities in clock towers have been perpetrated by modern architects in India.

Finally, we got to the gate of the old city of Lucknow, by which we entered the principal street of the bazaar. There were many interesting native shops. At one I noticed some blocks of patterns for printing by hand on cotton. They were cut in some hard wood. The handicraft, too, was still carried on here. There were many pretty bead necklaces, tassels, and quaint toys. We visited, up a steep narrow staircase, a muslin and jewel merchant's store. He showed some charming Indian

BETTER LUCK AT LUCKNOW—THROUGH THE CHOWK ON AN ELEPHANT

muslins spangled with silver spots and patterns. He also had one or two pieces of old Lucknow enamel not ordinarily seen in the bazaars now.

We visited another friend who had been spending the winter at Lucknow—Mrs Jopling-Rowe, the well-known artist, whose son is a Magistrate here, dining with them at their charming bungalow one evening. Mr Commissioner Jopling very courteously placed elephants at our disposal on which to ride through the chowk.

An irrigation well near the hotel interested me, and I made a sketch of it in a chequered shade. The yoke of oxen and two natives at work hauling up the water for the garden in a leather bucket. While thus engaged another friend travelling in the East came up, so that as regards friends we were quite in luck's way at Lucknow.

After this it was time to go and meet the elephants our friends had ordered at the chowk. Mrs Jopling-Rowe took us in her carriage through Wentworth Park, and past the palaces to the gate of the city, where we found two fine elephants in waiting. My wife and I mounted one of them by the usual ladder, the animal kneeling. A young officer who was of the party, however, showed us another way. He got a leg up by means of the trunk, and so over the elephant's head on to his back. We then processed through the bazaar (the chowk), preceded by a native policeman, in khaki with a scarlet turban, to clear the way, and two more behind. The elephants seemed to quite fill up the narrow street, so that there was danger of a block when we met an ox-cart. A very comprehensive view is to be had from an elephant's back, as one can see not only a long way ahead, but well into the shops where the people are at

IRRIGATION WELL, LUCKNOW

work, and also command the balconies and roofs, where there were often interesting groups.

We threaded our way through the chowk, passing at its end under one of the old arched gateways and along a narrower street, which led us out into the broad military road, which the British, after the revolt, ruthlessly cut right through the old city, uglifying it, of course. There is a wonderful variety and richness, again, here, in the old house-fronts with arcaded balconies and doorways of carved wood. The patterns, chiefly running borders, treated very fancifully and delicately. The native houses were not so high as in Lahore, but the carving might compare with the same sort of work there in detail.

We lunched at the charming abode of another English official and his wife (Mr and Mrs Saunders), who were very pleasant and hospitable. The lady had considerable taste in furniture and decoration, and her rooms showed the influence of white and green, and looked cool and agreeable in a light key.

Afterwards we drove to see the celebrated Martinière, the young officer accompanying us. The Martinière is the fantastic palace built by the French General or Captain Martin, before mentioned, and is a curious conglomerate sort of scenic design of late Italo-French Renaissance character, reminding one rather of Isola Bella, semi-classical figures being perched on every pinnacle and balustrade, and there were two grotesque lions, doing duty as supporters or consoles, with mouths so open that the sky could be seen through them. The building towered high in several stories in the centre, and spread out wide into two curved long and low wings of one story, opening on to broad terraces and steps leading to a small lake, from the middle of which rose a fluted column. The general's heart is said to be buried beneath this. The Martinière was intended by him to be a college for boys. He founded another at Calcutta, and another in his native town—Lyons—in France. Martin seems to have had a curious, eventful history, beginning as a French prisoner, under the British, afterwards entering the British army and becoming a captain, when he took service under the Nawab of Oudh and became general of his army, finally accumulating by some means a large fortune, which he spent on this building and in founding the schools which bear his name.

We passed another house ruined at the time of "the Mutiny," whence the women and children were removed to from the Residency, and where Lieutenant Paul is buried.

Mr Ross Scott entertained us with a distinguished company to dinner at his hospitable house before we left Lucknow. One English colonel of the party with whom I had a conversation had recently returned from Burmah, and had brought back some fine silk embroidered robes, some china bowls, and caps. The latter were of soft felt, and could be worn either with the edge turned down or up, forming a brim.

The colonel had lived some time in Burmah and had seen service there, having been through the British campaign against the "Dacoits." He said that the Dacoits were largely composed of men of the disbanded native army (for which I suppose our Government were responsible), and they roamed about the country preying on the people, plundering and sometimes murdering them. The Burmese people, he said, only wanted to be left alone in peace (like most people). He had made many friends among them, as he knew the language and had lived amongst them at that time. On revisiting the country and finding things under British control and administration, he found most of his Burmese native friends in prison. They were there, he said, merely for breaking some official regulation which probably they did not in the least understand. The natives complained to him that the English officials lived aloof from them, and were not friendly and sympathetic as he (the Colonel) had been, and they never got any forwarder.

CHAPTER XII

BENARES

OUR next destination was Benares. I had for long had the feeling, from the descriptions one had read and the photographs one had seen of this wonderful place, that it would sum up and centralise, as it were, to the eye the whole life of the Indian people, while it would also be a symbol of their faith to the mind.

It was, therefore, with unusual anticipations that we turned our faces thither, and on the 21st of January took the early morning train from Lucknow to the great focus of Hindu worship on the sacred Ganges. The kind commissioner's native servant, in scarlet, awaited us at the station with a parting gift and a note of introduction to the Maharajah of Benares.

The train passed through a richer and more fruitful country than usual, but level, plain all the way, reaching Benares Cantonment about two o'clock. We drove to Clark's hotel, which has a pretty portico full of palms, and a splendid orange creeper, then in full flower, hung over the usual bungalow annexe. The house was quiet, and had a semi-private aspect, more like a country bungalow.

Finding the Maharajah's palace was some five

or six miles off and on the other side of the river, we were advised to leave our letter at the Guest House with our cards. The Guest House was quite near by. Continuing our drive through the bazaar we thought the main street wider than most of the native cities, but the bazaars did not look so busy, and many shops were vacant. Balconies, the roofs of which were supported on arcades of slender columns with Hindu caps, were of a different type to those hitherto seen. In the European quarter there were poorly-designed, would-be Gothic British buildings, and mission churches of the usual bald type. There was a Queen's Park with the commonplace iron railing and low stone parapet enclosing it, these innovations, as usual, quite spoiling the surroundings of a native city.

The next morning we had a visit from the Maharajah's private secretary, who invited us to drive in the afternoon to visit the Buddhish topes and sculptures at Sarnath about five miles from Benares. An American lady we had previously met was to be of the party, and she was staying at the Guest House, and at the appointed hour the Maharajah's carriage, with a coachman in a green and gold turban and scarlet tunic, and two active young Hindus, similarly dressed, acted as running footmen to clear the way, when not at their posts standing at the back of the carriage. We called at the Guest House for our American friend. It was a more palatial building than the one at Gwalior, standing in a small park with outer gates and a drive. The house was in the classic style—a white building with flat roof and columned portico. In the large hall on the ground floor there was a small coloured statuette of the Maharajah on

THE MAHARAJAH PLACES HIS CARRIAGE AT OUR DISPOSAL

horseback, photographs and portraits upon the walls, including English miniatures of an English officer and his ladies of the early nineteenth century, and some engravings of portraits of Queen Caroline. A stuffed lioness was lying on a side-board.

The road to Sarnath lay through avenues of fine trees a great part of the way, chiefly mangoes, banyans, acacias, and tamarinds. The young trees planted to fill the gaps were protected by circular fences, sometimes topped by prickly pears. Sometimes the circular fence was made of bricks, an aperture being left between every alternate brick.

At Sarnath we saw the results of recent excavations. There was a wonderful pillar made out of a single piece of marble, but fractured in digging it out. One part stood upright in the earth, the other lay horizontally. The top or cap was placed under an awning near by. It was formed of four lions facing outwards, their heads, chests, and fore limbs being alone visible, their claws resting on the rim of a circular fillet, on which was sculptured in low relief a horse, an elephant, a lion, and a bull, each animal being placed between a wheel of a solar character, each wheel having twenty-four spokes. Below this fillet was a curved drooping fringe of leaves such as are characteristic in Persian columns as well as Hindu. The marble of which the column and the sculptures were made was of a peculiar greyish almost of a flesh colour, with small spots. Both the column and the sculptures were very highly polished, and the treatment of the lions was remarkably Greek in character with perhaps a touch of Persian or even Assyrian formalism in the treatment of the heads and manes of the lions. The animals in relief, between the wheels, too, were remarkably free, spirited, and well modelled.

There were the remains of an ancient Buddhist temple near. In what was probably the inner shrine was a sculptured standing figure of Buddha, about two-thirds life size, in alto relievo. The figure was represented in a long robe, the limbs being boldly expressed through the drapery, which hung broadly and smoothly over them, without folds, except at the sides, which were treated in the rather formal spiral manner of early Greek work.

The American lady remarked on seeing this figure that "The gentleman seems to have put his legs through his clothes."

The figure was framed in a border of astralagus, cut in low relief, having a running escalloped border outside it and stepped mouldings. The doorway to this shrine, too, had a richly carved bordering.

There were many most interesting fragments collected together in and around a building near. In the court was a large circular carved stone. This was called Buddha's umbrella, and its original position was over the head of a large figure of the saint, sculptured in the round, close by. The design of the umbrella, a lotus flower, the flower of life, the petals radiating from the centre, and enclosing this were a series of concentric rings of pattern; the first consisted of rosettes, or smaller lotus flowers, alternating with grotesque lions, winged horses, elephants, camels, and bulls; the next showed the anthemion, doubled or reversed, alternating with the fylfot or gammadion 卐, and another form frequent in early Greek pattern (as well as Chinese) the geometric four-petalled flower. There were numerous small figures of Buddha here, treated in a similar way to the one first mentioned, as well as other sculptures of a Hindu type, resembling those at Ellora.

There we saw the great Tope (called the Dhamek). This stood on rather higher ground, and was apparently built of rubble, which was exposed at the top, but the sides were covered with fine bands of carved ornament in stone, carried to a considerable height, and consisting of a frieze of bold scroll work of a Greek character, alternating with bands of a kind of Chinese-like diagonal diaper, divided by plain belts of stone. At intervals these bands were intersected by flat dome-shaped forms slightly projecting beyond the bands, and in these were recesses intended, no doubt, originally to contain seated figures of Buddha. These flat dome-shaped forms, connected by bands, suggested a palisade, which may have been the original way of enclosing and protecting these topes or tombs; and they may also have been the early form or prototype of the curious clustered dome-shaped pinnacles which are multiplied to form the spires of Jain temples so often seen in India.

Sarnath is the place where Buddha began to preach, and the great tope is supposed to mark the spot where his first sermon was delivered. The excavations of General Cunningham here disclose the fragments of a great city which probably stood here about 2000 years ago.

Returning to Benares from this intensely interesting spot, we dined at the Guest House with our American friend. The rooms were luxuriously upholstered and furnished from Europe, and were occupied by the Prince and Princess of Wales when they were here in 1905. The dinner was excellently cooked and served by native attendants, with the choicest wines and liquors.

There were some lovely old Indian miniatures on vellum framed and hanging on the wall of one of the salons, representing various scenes in the life of a Maharajah—a cock-fight, polo, reception of a foreign embassy (in Dutch seventeenth century costume), and other subjects, each full of charming details of architecture, dress and decoration. Besides these there were the usual official photographic groups, showing English officers, princes, and governor-generals grouped around the Maharajah—in one the Czar of Russia appeared. Indian carpets were on the floor, and English sporting prints on the walls of the dining-room.

The next day, January 23rd, His Highness's secretary had arranged to send a carriage for us quite early (about 7 A.M.), to take us to see the ghats. When we reached the river side, which is a considerable drive from the Guest House, we found a beautiful state barge awaiting us. It was shaped and painted like a peacock, and had a little pavilion in the centre. In this lovely vessel we embarked, and glided slowly down the river with the stream, guided by the scarlet-jacketed oarsmen, with their long bamboo handled oars, and a broad steering paddle at the stern.

The spectacle of Benares from a boat on the Ganges is perhaps the most extraordinary sight in all India. At every ghat or opening to the river, down the great flights of steps, a throng of natives in all the colours of the rainbow press to the water's

BENARES: VIEWING THE GHATS FROM THE MAHARAJAH'S PEACOCK BOAT

edge. Some plunge in, some approach timidly, and very gradually submerge themselves. Their brown skins shining in the water. The men always have some sort of waist cloth on, but the women go in in their garments, or, at least, clad to their waists. All ages are there—it recalled the mediæval allegories of the Fountain of Youth. One does not often see infants dipped, though they are, occasionally, by their parents, and object to the water in the same natural and vigorous manner as European babies are apt to do at their baptism.

Old tottering women and men may be seen, as well as the young, strong and vigorous, all earnestly washing, or performing strange genuflexions with the most determined devotion. Characteristic features of this wonderful scene are the large matting umbrellas of the priests, who sit on small platforms of bamboo raised on the steps. These expect fees to be paid them by those who come to bathe at the ghats. Rows of snake charmers greet the traveller on landing at the ghats, who turn hissing cobras out of circular boxes and hold them aloft or twine them round their necks, or perhaps, as an extra attraction, empty out a swarm of scorpions to catch the eye of the stranger, all eager to perform the marvels of their art on the slightest encouragement—and a few rupees. Sacred zebu bulls wander about and often lie on the steps.

It seems strange that people should lave and drink of the water, which is fouled one would suppose by all sorts of impurities at the margin. Washing of clothes goes on everywhere, decayed flowers float along, even bodies of drowned dogs are seen occasionally. It must have been at Benares that Æsop's fable of the two pots was born, for there the earthen and brazen vessels might quite possibly float down the stream together. Pots are scoured on the steps, and at the Burning Ghat they pour the ashes of the dead into the river.

At the Burning Ghat they pile up logs of wood to

WE SEE SNAKES AT BENARES

form the pyre, and the white turbaned dark figures, with nothing on but waist cloths, are kept busy at their ghastly work. Some of the bodies are brought down with flowers and chanting : others lie there with no following or ceremony : some are swathed in red or white cloth like mummies, others as they were born are lifted on to the piles of logs, which being set alight, soon reduce all to the same condition.

Some of the bodies are carefully dipped in the Ganges before being burned, and are often left at the water's edge while the pyre is being prepared. Wood was placed over as well as under the bodies, and a torch was put to the mouth. Other bodies, again, are taken out in boats unburned and apparently dressed and seated in chairs, and suddenly in mid-stream are toppled over into the water. We saw an old man disposed of in this way. Our boatman pointed him out as a specially holy person, and we did not realise he was a corpse. The bodies of infants, swathed in white, are also treated in this way.

The Maharajah's secretary explained that the Ganges water had been analysed by European experts and pronounced to be the best water in the world, having a peculiar property of destroying the germs of disease. It was difficult, however, to see how even "the best water" could avoid getting fouled with such operations constantly going on; but of course there is a strong stream all the time, so that everything must eventually be carried down to the sea.

A continuous many-coloured stream of pilgrims, bearing huge bundles of bedding, were constantly moving along behind this busy life of the bathing ghats, ascending or descending the great flights of steps leading up through the various gates to the city. It seemed to be part of that universal exodus we had witnessed at every railway station in India. It is said that representatives from every village in the peninsula may be found at Benares.

Then, as a no less striking background to these extraordinary human groups, rise the domes of temples and minarets of palaces, their golden vanes and finials glittering against the deep blue sky. Windows, balconies and terraces placed high up, with vast walls below them. These great walls, which give so much distinction and breadth to the river front of Benares, have a practical reason, inasmuch as it is a necessity thus to raise the temple and palace floors, owing to the sudden rising of the Ganges in the rainy season, when these walls are sometimes hidden in the waters.

The musical accompaniments of the spectacle consist in the weird and wandering notes which issue from the temples, produced by a sort of hautboy, and the subdued thud of the tomtoms. I saw a dusky long-haired fakir stand on the steps at the Mahikarunika ghat and sound a long straight brass trumpet.

After voyaging in the peacock boat the whole length of the ghats, we returned to our carriage-in-waiting at a convenient point from which to approach the Golden Temple. From the main street of the Bazaar we were conducted by the secretary down a very narrow passage crowded with worshippers, and then up a dark staircase to a terrace from which we could see the cluster of gilded copper domes. Afterwards in the sacred precincts we saw the "well of knowledge," but did not drink of it, having too much foreknowledge of the condition of its water.

Our next excursion was to pay a visit to the Maharajah at his palace. We were conducted by his secretary in the carriage as before, driving to the river side opposite the palace some six miles off. On the road we stopped to see the famous Monkey Temple—a Hindu Temple in an arcaded court of the usual type. This court was full of monkeys—a sandy-brown coloured sort with pink faces, probably Macaques—not so handsome as the wild silver grey ones we had seen at Ahmelabad. They accepted offerings, but not so greedily, as they were evidently well fed, and dried peas lay about untouched. They gambolled about the temple at their sweet will. These monkeys are sacred to Vishnu, and represent Hunuman the monkey god.

There was a fine tank with steps to the water's edge, close by the temple. Just before this we passed the Hindu College which Mrs Annie Besant has established for the higher education of native children of both sexes—but not a mixed school. This work has been liberally endowed by the Maharajah of Benares, who also granted the site. Mrs Besant is the principal, but owing to the illness of Colonel Alcott, she was not then there, being at Madras nursing the Colonel in what proved to be his last illness.

Reaching the river side, a boat was in waiting to take us across to the palace, rowed by two Hindu boys—at least they started rowing, but soon we got into shallows, where they took to poling, and finally had to get out and push the boat along, until getting into deeper water again they rowed us to the palace steps.

It was quite a high steep flight, no doubt existing

for the same river reason as the high walls of Benares—to be out of the reach of the floods. There were numbers of natives ascending and descending or grouped on the steps.

We climbed up, and entered the palace up more stairs, and were shown into a large reception salon, where much of the furniture was "under canvas," but there was one handsome couch displayed, inlaid with ivory. Presently H.H. the Maharajah entered, accompanied by his two chief officers, who spoke English well, his painter in ordinary, and several attendants. Chairs were placed in the centre of the room, around a small marble table. The Maharajah seated himself, and we with the private secretary grouped ourselves about him. The Maharajah was dressed in a small-patterned long tunic of pink brocaded with gold, a small round cap on his head, close fitting white trousers and patent leather shoes. He seemed quite merry and pleased to see us. I showed him my book of sketches, which interested him, as he said he had never seen drawings of the kind before. His painter in ordinary, to whom I was introduced, was also interested, and asked some questions through the secretary, not himself speaking English. He had painted the full length portraits of the Maharajahs which hung aloft in this salon. The Prince presently rose and invited us to the terrace, to which we passed after him, through an arcade, an attendant holding a large silk umbrella over him. There was a very fine view from this terrace up and down the river. The city of Benares, with its domes and minarets, seen far down on the left, and the open plain country opposite. The secretary said that when the Ganges rose the city looked as if it was floating on the surface of the water.

We then all returned to the salon (or Durbar Hall,

THE MAHARAJAH'S RECEPTION, DECORATING THE VISITORS

as I ought to have called it) and took our leave, H.H. presenting us with a book of photographs of the ghats, with his own portrait, both of which he inscribed. Finally he placed necklaces of some kind of gold or gilt tissue around the necks of the ladies, and one of silver-tissue around mine, and concluded by putting scent on our handkerchiefs from a handsome silver bottle.

Before we left the palace the Maharajah's jewels

were shown to us—wonderful strings of rubies and emeralds almost as big as hen's eggs. These were in rather worn and faded cases of velvet, and offered up on rusty old tea trays—a strange mixture of splendour and squalor.

The secretary then took us by carriage to see a Hindu Temple, covered with sculpture, standing clear on a raised platform ascended by a flight of steps, and surrounded by the usual open court. We saw several fine elephants waiting at a gateway, and afterwards visited the Maharajah's pleasant flower garden, prettily laid out with long centre tanks, and rose trellises, terraces, and pavilions. From here we soon reached the river side, and embarking in the boat again, returned in the same manner we had come, returning to our quarters in the dusk of the evening, the secretary leaving us at his dwelling at Benares.

The Maharajah having placed a boat and a carriage at our disposal, we arranged to visit the ghats again the next day, especially as I was anxious to obtain a sketch or two of the wonderful scenes by the river. So driving to the steps again we embarked, taking Moonsawmy with us to interpret. I got the boatmen to stop the boat off the Manikaranika Ghat,[1] which is perhaps the most striking of all, with its red sandstone pinnacles, immense flights of steps and terraces. Here I worked till noon, when one had rather the sensation of everything curling up with the heat of the sun, including one's own frame! The next morning we again returned to the river, using the Maharajah's carriage

[1] See frontispiece.

and boat, which latter was not, however, the beautiful peacock barge of our first morning, but a very substantial sort of house-boat, with plenty of space on the upper deck or flat roof of the house, and solid chairs to sit on. This time I chose the Nepal Temple for my subject. This temple, with its pagoda-like roof and shining golden finial, had a Chinese aspect. The temple itself was of a deep rich Indian red, and had a terrace in front on the top of a high wall close to the river, on one side being the entrance to the palace with two minarets. A mass of dark green foliage partly shaded the Temple on the left hand and added to the charm and richness of the subject—the throng of figures on the steps, and the boats rocking on the clear green water, completing the picture at the river's edge, alive with colour and movement. The procession of pilgrims in an endless line, and the whole human drama going on just as before, and as it has been every day for ages.

The moon was now again bright at nights and it was much warmer. We heard the jackals again as at Udaipur.

We met two London friends at the hotel, and made some pleasant acquaintances—a young American who had been travelling in China and Japan and Java and was going on to Europe; also three young Oxford men, connected with the Oxford Mission, I understood—one of them on his way to take up some official post in Japan.

The roses at Clark's Hotel were very profuse, a beautiful silver bowl of Benares work full of them each day decorated our table.

It was extremely quiet except for the almost continual cry of a bird I could not name, but which at first we thought was a pea-fowl. The note, however, was not hoarse or grating but full and bell-like, though very monotonous, consisting of two notes. We heard this bird everywhere south after Benares.

CHAPTER XIII

CALCUTTA—DARJEELING

WITH parting compliments to the Maharajah, whom I ventured to present, and his officers, with photographs of some of my pictures, we left Benares for Calcutta on January 26th, departing by a mid-day train, belated as usual. This took us to Mogul Serai, where we changed into the Calcutta mail. At the station it was difficult to find a place for the soles of our feet, as the whole of the platform was occupied by native infantry, in khaki, who were camping down with their arms piled and their baggage around them.

The Calcutta mail was preceded by the limited mail, consisting chiefly of post-office vans, but having room for a few passengers. One of our friends of the Oxford party who were going on by it very kindly tried to get us places also, but there was no room left. However, the other mail followed very quickly, in which we found plenty of room, our only fellow-traveller being an American.

We had, before reaching Mogul Serai, obtained a farewell glimpse of Benares as we crossed the iron bridge over the Ganges, below the city, and saw the slender minarets of the Aurangzer Mosque, and the smoke of the Burning Ghat. The country for some distance was richer and more fruitful than usual, and well clad with trees, among which were many fine cocoa palms, their smooth, slender stems having a steely blue effect against the deep green foliage of mangoes and acacias.

The scenery grew tamer afterwards, and generally flat, with occasional mud-walled and thatch-roofed villages huddled together.

After passing as bad a night as might be expected in the train, we got into Calcutta about six in the morning at the Howrah station.

After some difficulty in getting a tickorgary—the Indian equivalent for a "four-wheeler"—we had rather a long drive to the Grand Hotel, crossing the river by a bridge just outside the station, where there was a bathing ghat, gaily populous at that hour, the bathing operations being followed by breakfast on the steps or in the pavilions on the terrace behind.

The streets of Calcutta looked rather dingy and neglected. The hotel was vast but gloomy, and the prices high; but a bath and a rest after the long railway journey were very welcome, and we were glad to get our letters. We found the temperature much warmer, however, and more like Bombay.

The Minto Fête—a sort of bazaar and military tournament combined—absorbed a great deal of attention among the residents. This occupied a large enclosure on the Esplanade, under canvas. The familiar posters used for the Military Tournament in London met the eye on all sides, with gay fluttering bunting strung across the streets as it appeared the Amir was expected here too, though his visit was to be considered "private."

One of our introductions here was to Miss Sorabji, a Parsee lady of much influence, and a

THE SOOTHSAYER AT CALCUTTA—(OR PALMISTRY UNDER THE PALMS)

most interesting personality, well known and beloved by a large circle of English friends. She had a charming house, in a garden of palms, in Carnac Street. We found her entertaining a party of fashionable ladies at afternoon tea, on a shady lawn in front of her house. In the midst of the group, squatting on the grass, was a soothsayer and palmist—a Hindu "wise man," robed in white, but without any turban. He had some oblong-shaped pages out of an ancient book of palmistry, and some curious phrenological-looking diagrams lying on the grass in front of him, and these he appeared to be consulting from time to time, while with great deliberation he examined the hands of the ladies, who gazed at him quite anxiously, as if he were really an inspired diviner of their lives. This man was supposed to be gifted with very special powers, and seemed to be taken quite seriously, but as far as we could gather, he was only mentioning the usual range of probable or not impossible events which might happen in the course of any life, though, no doubt, more or less adapted to the circumstances and character of the lady before him, as far as he could guess it, and calculated to fit individual cases. He certainly looked wily and cunning enough for anything, as he moved his finger mysteriously over the charts, or pretended to count or reckon something while keeping the lady's left hand open before him. A curious scene altogether, with the afternoon tea-table, and the ordinary chatter going on.

There was an Industrial Exhibition open on some open ground near a large, yellow-washed, eighteenth century style of church. It combined a switchback railway, and some of the popular attractions of Earl's Court, with an interesting show of hand-weaving in linens, silks, and carpets, with dyeing, printing, and other industries, the exhibits being those of societies or firms. In some cases the work of various schools of Art were shown, as that of the Maharajah's, at Jaipur, chiefly metal work and enamelling. Among the brass work were to be seen the spherical brass rolling lamps, pierced with an all-over intricate floral design, that left fairly evenly distributed apertures through which the rays of light would strike when the lamp was lighted within. This, by an ingenious piece of mechanism, always maintained its level position, though the sphere might be rolled along the ground like a ball. It could be opened by hinges in two equal hemispherical halves. These lamps are used at festivals in the temples, and have a beautiful effect.

Calcutta is not impressive architecturally, certainly. The modern buildings are of the usual commercial type as a rule. Government House has a certain stateliness with its white columned porticoes among the palms and greenery of other trees ; and Carnac Street is a long wide street of large detached residences standing in ample gardens. The Esplanade is a wide open plain in the midst of the town, with some groups of trees upon it, but rather brown and desolate, the turf being burned by the sun. The native quarters are very squalid. The bazaars and shops were often tumble-down temporary-looking sheds and structures of bamboo sticks and straw, old tins being often seen thrown on to weight the rotten matting or thatch which formed the roofs, which were often, too, patched with corrugated iron. Occasionally there was a house-front which had seen better days—a former villa or mansion, with a columned portico, but now become a squalid tenement house.

These were at least one's impressions on a very short visit; but it was so oppressive that we were anxious to get away to Darjeeling, and so took our departure on January 28th by an afternoon train from the Iscaldah station. For about an hour or so after leaving Calcutta, the train runs through beautiful groves of palms and mangoes, plantains and bamboos, intersected by tanks of water, vegetable gardens, and thatched villages among the trees. Later we crossed the great open plains of Bengal, cultivated and fertile under irrigation, with but few trees, stretching as far as the eye could see under the full moon.

At Sara we changed, having to leave the train to cross the river Ganges. The scene was a strange one. The waiting steamer lying ready, had to be approached over the wide shallows by two long narrow gangways, constructed out of a few planks, suspended from bamboo sticks stuck upright in the shallow water, with lights at intervals. A troop of European and American travellers wending their way from the train along one of the gangways to the white steamer, and a procession of natives with their bundles crowding along the other to the same vessel.

Arrived on board we found a table spread ready on the quarter-deck and we had an excellent dinner—very superior to those provided by most of the hotels. After this meal was over the steamer started on its voyage across the wide river, having a strong electric search-light at the bows which threw a great shaft of white light to the opposite shore, along which it seemed to travel as if finding its way. Moths and flying insects fluttering into the beam of light flashed like sparks or fire-flies.

We found another train waiting for us at a station on the other bank. Here we got into sleeping compartments. I had an American bishop and his friend, a young man, as travelling companions. About 6 A.M. the next morning we reached the foot of the hills, where another change was necessary and where breakfast was to be had at the station, after which we packed ourselves and our belongings into the tiny carriages of the little narrow gauge, toy-like train which makes the ascent of 7000 feet to Darjeeling.

Starting about level, the ascent was quite gradual at first, the line winding through bamboo groves and tea plantations, and as it grows steeper the track twists up in S curves and loops, threading, like a steel snake, through umbrageous woodlands, sometimes following the road, sometimes crossing it. Among the many beautiful trees there was one of frequent occurrence which was new to us. It had something the manner of growth of an ash, but having a silvery bark like a birch, and clusters of large scarlet buds and flowers, without leaves. Some called it the "Forest Flame." Many of the trees were hung with climbing plants, forming lovely tangles and festoons, and through the openings in the woods, here and there, we had glimpses of the plains veiled in the morning haze. Higher and higher the little train carried us, curving so sharply, sometimes, that one could see the little puffing engine in front, which had almost the effect, when rounding the sudden curves and loops, of some grotesque creature trying to catch its own tail, like a playful kitten or puppy!

At intervals the various attitudes attained were

THE DARJEELING TOY-RAILWAY TRYING TO CATCH ITS OWN TAIL!

painted on tablets at the side of the rail, or at the little stations. At Siliguri a halt was made for tiffin. Here the Mongolian and Bhutian peasants came up to the railway carriages and offered us interesting things in the way of silver rings, and silver ornaments set with turquoise, and large turquoise earrings of a fine bold design. The women all wore relic or charm-boxes with lids worked in delicate filigree and set with turquoise, and these were suspended by bead necklaces. Silver chatelaines and other charming ornaments were shown us, the women carrying the stock-in-trade of jewellery upon their persons. The high cheek-bones and narrow eyes, black hair and long pig-tails of the Mongolian were very marked, the men having quite a Chinese look, with their soft felt, turned-up inverted cup-and-saucer-shaped hats and pig-tails. The women had broad, smiling faces, the effect of which was heightened by a kind of bright brown varnish which made their faces look as if they had been French polished—perhaps to suit somebody's furniture?—their hair was intensely black, and they wore two long plaits or pig-tails.

The huts of the villages were of wood, and the original native roofing was of thin wooden shingles, which harmonised perfectly with the scenery; but unfortunately corrugated iron was being extensively substituted for roofing purposes, and the old thatch or wooden shingles were frequently patched with it. At Darjeeling it was almost universal, and in consequence the buildings might be described as tin and temporary. Here and there was a fantastic, but generally not tasteful, touch of Germany, or the Swiss border, in the modern villa. Little toy-like dwellings are scattered along the mountain-sides in an accidental sort of way, as if they had been upset out of a box, and had stuck here and there among the trees in their fall.

English suburban names catch the eye—at Darjeeling—such as "Daisy Bank" and "Rose Cottage." The Europeans come out from Calcutta in the hot season to dwell here. The huts of the native people look very frail, almost like card-houses, leaning up against each other on the edges of cliffs, their roofs of ragged matting, straw thatch, or thin wooden shingles, or the corrugated iron aforesaid. Tall, tapering bamboo canes are frequently stuck up outside, bearing vertical strips of white cotton or linen cloth, like standards, with light tags of the same fluttering at intervals from their outer edges. These are said to represent prayers, and are supposed to ward off evil influences

We put up at "Woodlands" hotel, which has a pretty walk up from the station, lined with fine old trees of the pine kind, very thick and dark, and having a slender cone-like form, reminding one of cypresses. These abound all down the mountain-sides, but are now in danger of being thinned too freely. The mountain-sides are intersected with paths, and terraced bridle roads, along which are perched the dwellings, above or below the road. As one rides up one can look almost perpendicularly down upon the tin roofs and into the little gardens, as these paths almost double back on themselves at different heights, as they wind up the hills.

The manager and proprietor of "Woodlands" was an Italian by birth, but he spoke English like a native. He was one of an expedition which attempted to climb the Kinchin Junga (18,000 feet), a great snow peak of the Himalayas, which is conspicuous from Darjeeling when the clouds disclose the view of the wonderful snow-clad range.

He occasionally entertained his guests by a lecture in the evenings, illustrated by photographic slides taken on the expedition (in 1905) in which,

CHARACTERS IN A TIBETAN MASQUE, DARJEELING

however, four of the party lost their lives by losing their footing on a snow precipice. Climbing in the Himalayas seems to be handicapped by the necessity of taking coolies to carry provisions and camp furniture, as the explorer leaves the human world entirely behind him in entering these trackless snow-bound solitudes.

One evening, just before daylight had quite faded, we witnessed a very curious and remarkable performance in the courtyard of the hotel, lighted by a few lanterns, which, however, rather increased the mystery of the half-light than really added to the illumination of the scene. It was a Tibetan dance or masque. To the sound of tom-toms, which marked the time, a dancer in loose white garments appeared—a man; he wore a white tunic with a full skirt, and held a sort of white veil up over his head as he moved, and he appeared to have on Mongolian leggings and boots. He danced like a dervish, whirling rapidly round and round, his skirts forming a sort of spiral wheel of drapery about him as he moved.

This dancer having finished his *pas de seul*, as a kind of prelude, retired, and was immediately succeeded by another—a fantastic-looking figure also in white, with the Tibetan conical turban, the details of whose costume I could not quite make out, owing to the fitful light, but he appeared in the characteristic loose tunic and leggings and the Chinese-like shoes. His style of dancing was quite different to the dervish, and might be described as a combination of the jig and the reel. While he was dancing there entered two very grotesque Chinese-looking lions, queer monsters, made up of two people who furnished the four legs—probably a man for the fore-quarters and a boy for the hindmost. Their heads or masks seemed to be each formed of half a tortoise shell, ingeniously enough the openings at the side of the shell being utilised as the sockets of large fierce staring eyes, a large open red mouth, and gleaming rows of pointed white teeth, completing a terrific countenance. Yellow drapery concealed all but the feet, which were clad in some kind of tawny soft leather. These lions were extremely lively, and frisked about, and lashed their tails in a most spirited way, keeping time with the tom-toms through all their wild movements; as, together with the second dancer, who was, it appeared, the lion-tamer, they went through a very active and energetic dance. This over, each lion lay down, one on one side of the ground (there being no stage), and one on the other, facing the audience as they couched.

Then entered a sort of knight, or warrior, on a red hobby-horse, and the dance was continued by his chasing the lion-tamer round and round, the latter always eluding his pursuer, and always emphatically repeating by the action of his arms the beat of the tom-toms in a defiant sort of way.

Six more hobby-horsed riders in different costumes and colours next came in, one after the other, and joined in the pursuit of the lion-tamer. Presently, however, they changed the figure, the red hobby-horse remaining stationary, while the other six formed a sort of quadrille, advancing and retiring, and crossing over, as in the opening figure of "the Lancers." I forget exactly how the lion-tamer employed himself while this proceeded, but I think he must have temporarily subsided, while the hobby-horses kept the attention of the audience. Finally they all joined hands and danced in a ring, raising a curious kind of chant the while, after which the hobby-horses all marched out in single file, still chanting.

Then a peacock (with a skirt) came in, moving in a slow, measured and stately fashion, dancing and bowing in a quaint manner, flapping its wings occasionally; next it approached one of the couchant lions, who all this while had remained passive, and apparently sleeping, and gave it a sudden and decisive peck, the action being instantly emphasised by the tom-toms. After more genuflexions the peacock finished his dance by giving a similar peck to the other lion, each lion at the touch starting violently and lashing their tails. Then exit the peacock.

Next appeared, crawling in with a sort of wobble, a turtle, also wearing a skirt which concealed its feet. At its entry the lion-tamer exhibited all the symptoms of comic fear, trying to hide himself from the turtle, and finally as it approached nearer, he threw himself on the ground and wriggled and writhed about in an access of ridiculous terror. Presently, however, whatever had animated the interior of the turtle it vanished unperceived, and the shell lay motionless on the ground. The lion-tamer approaching it apprehensively, but eventually taking up the shell, he danced up to the lions, who sprang to their feet, and then all these whirled about in a wild tempestuous dance to double quick time, until the lions, apparently exhausted, both lay down again in the same order as before. Again the troops of hobby-horses entered, and after another spin with the lion-tamer, all marched out, chanting, the beat of the tom-toms gradually growing fainter till they ceased as the company disappeared.

We had not yet been favoured with a glimpse of the great snow peaks. Kinchin Junga seemed extremely shy, and remained wrapped in impenetrable folds of cloud which rolled over the edges of the narrow hills, or steamed up from the deep valleys, enacting the constant-inconstant drama of cloud and mountain, always a most fascinating spectacle. On January 30th, however, in the morning, between seven and eight, we were at last rewarded by a beautiful glimpse of the snow peaks of the Himalayas, dominated by that of Kinchin Junga, clear in the golden light of early morning, piercing the turquoise sky, like the vision of some celestial city floating on a sea of roseate cloud. The unusual height of the peaks in the sky surprised the eye, accustomed to see clouds where now were these vast mountains. The delicate modelling of the snow summits clear and sharp in the sunlight had the effect of making them look much nearer than the intervening valleys and dark pine covered slopes lost in mist and deep shadow, and it was strange to think that one gazed at these snow peaks across a distance of about 45 miles.

Human dwellings and structures looked flimsy and trifling, no more than the work of ants or spiders, comparatively speaking, but indeed

KINCHIN JUNGA FROM DARJEELING

Darjeeling has no architecture to boast of. For a region subject to earthquakes great allowances must necessarily be made, but the corrugated iron style

THE SHY PEAK OF KINCHIN JUNGA

certainly failed to assert the dignity of man in such a landscape, and the native hut did not look more permanent or substantial than a bird's nest.

The little town has a central square where there

is a native market. Little low bazaars line the

A RIDE AT DARJEELING: "UP HILL SPARE ME"

sides, and the streets, but in the centre the vendors spread out their stock-in-trade on the bare ground. There may be seen turquoises in great quantity, and unset stones of many kinds, and an infinitude of silver rings and ornaments. The best, however, were always offered by the country people and the coolies, and the Bhutian women, who always seemed able to produce any number, and we were followed by quite a little crowd holding out rings and silver ornaments to tempt us, when we went through the market. My wife discovered a pair of green pigeons in a characteristic Indian domed-cage made of canes, hanging outside one of the native huts, and sent our bearer to negiotate the purchase, and for six rupees they changed hands. The birds travelled with us to Ceylon, and on the steamer homewards till we met the cold weather in the Mediterranean, when the hen bird died, the cock surviving until we reached Italy. They had to be fed upon a sort of meal made from a kind of powdered dried peas, not always easily obtainable.

There were many interesting walks and rides at Darjeeling. A favourite excursion was to Tiger Hill, a distance of six miles, from where Mount Everest, the highest mountain of the world, can be seen—in fine clear weather, and sunrise is the usual time for it. The modes of progression are by jin-rickshaws or ponies. There are excellent ponies to be had at Woodlands, and we enjoyed the steepest ride we had ever experienced.

The pig-tailed Mongolian coolies are always on hand in the courtyard of the hotel, waiting for custom in either mode of transport. Palanquins are also used.

We met here some English friends and fellow-travellers. It was pleasant to fall in with my old Bostonian friend, Mr Louis Prang, who, with Mrs

Prang, were travelling with a party of some twelve Bostonians.

The alarming accounts of the prevalence of small-pox at Bhutia deterred us from going to see the

A HAILSTONE CHORUS—DEPARTURE FROM DARJEELING

Buddhist temple at Bhutia Busti, though the immediate cause was a thunder-storm, which came on just as the rickshaws had been ordered, and stopped our excursion; and being advised to abandon the project for the reason above given we made no second attempt.

Before leaving Darjeeling we were favoured by another clear vision of the snow peaks and Kinchin Junga in all his glory, before breakfast, and I was glad to have been able to secure two drawings as a record of that wonderful view. We departed on the first of February in a hail-storm, walking down to the station in a pelting shower of enormous stones, which rattled around us with a thunder and lightning accompaniment. The hail-stones are so large sometimes in that district, and the storms so violent, that much damage is done. At Woodlands all the glass windows here on one occasion were broken, we heard; and also that the stones were known to have been occasionally large enough to kill deer!

We were soon on our way, joggling down to the plains again in the squeezy little train, the hail turning to rain lower down, and we were sometimes wrapped in cloud. As we got still lower, however, the sky towards the north-west began to clear, and there was a striking effect as of a great curtain being lifted up, showing the bright sky beyond and the sun shining on the plains. Soon we passed into his light again, and enjoyed clear weather to his setting.

Reversing in the course of our journey the changes, we proceeded to Sara again, recrossing the Ganges, the search-light producing striking effects as it wandered over the shore and the vessels, picking out its twin white steamer with startling distinctness. We had the morning light over the fruitful plains of Bengal, in which the scarlet flowering trees or "forest flame" before spoken of looked more wonderful than ever. The thatched huts of the native villages were interesting in shape, and differed from any other local variety we had seen. They were built of bamboo, with curving roof ridges. Groups of these huts were of frequent occurrence; they stood on raised platforms, interspersed with plantains, or date or cocoa palms, the window openings on the inward side only, and under the deep overhanging eaves.

CHAPTER XIV

MADRAS AND THE SOUTH

AVAILING ourselves of the kind hospitality of our friend in Carnac Street, we reposed during the day intending to leave Calcutta again by the night train (Madras Mail) for Madras, our next destination. This was a considerable journey as a glance at the map will show; in fact it was our longest in India, occupying two nights and two days.

After some anxious moments in Carnac Street, through our tickorgary not turning up for us at the time ordered, or through some muddling on the part of our bearer, we eventually got conveyed to Howrah Station. Luckily the train did not start so soon as stated—it never does in India—and we were saved.

The train proved, however, to be very crowded, and we could only secure a berth each in separate compartments, though there was a small sliding door between the ladies' and the gentlemen's sleeping compartment, through which communication could be made. Four ladies, a baby, and a parrot, and the green pigeons made up the complement in the ladies' part. I had two travelling companions only, a river-steamer captain or engineer on sick leave, going south with his family, and an English officer of the Army Medical Service going to some hill station beyond Madras. The former kept himself going with whiskey and soda, of which he freely

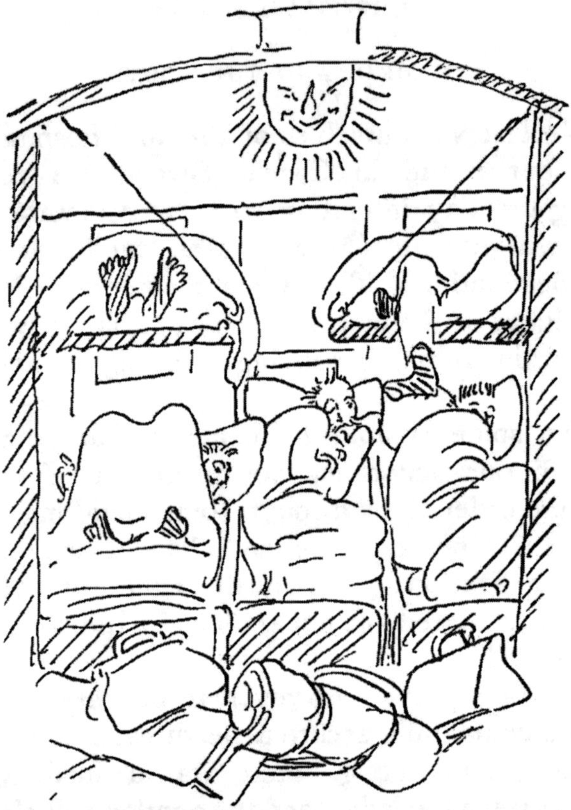

CALCUTTA TO MADRAS—SECTION OF SLEEPER—OR SOMETHING LIKE IT

invited his fellow travellers to partake. The latter proved to be Capt. J. B. Dalzell Hunter of the 64th pioneers. He was studying Persian, and introduced me to a most interesting book, the "IQD-I-GUL," or "The Rose Necklace," being selections from the Gulistan and auwār-i-suhaite translated into literal English with notes by Adāl-at Khan. This was full of delightful stories, and rich with oriental imagery and wisdom.

Leaving Calcutta in the darkness of night, of course nothing could be seen of the country till next morning when we were approaching Cuttack, when we took "Chota Hazri"—or early light breakfast. A little south of this hills appeared inland reminding one in character and apparent height of our lake country. We passed Poori, the junction for Juggernath, where crowds of pilgrims go, especially at the time of the great festival of Krishna in March, when the image of the god is borne through the town on the famous car, out to a temple in the country. The old story we were told in childhood of the dreadful heathen custom of the natives on such occasions throwing themselves under the wheels of the car of Juggernath has been discredited. Krishna, being a god of love and life, not a destroyer, would not be pleased with human sacrifices, and they would be quite inappropriate. It might be possible, however, that the car, drawn as it is by men with great cables, through the press of pilgrims, might accidentally crush some one fallen in the crowd, and European missionaries may have misunderstood what had really happened, and had misrepresented and exaggerated it.

There were many new and different types of natives at the stations. We were now on the Bengal-Nagpur Railway, and the native crowds, and groups entering or leaving the train all down the line, were most interesting in character and colour. Pilgrims from Juggernaut bearing small canes back with them as signs of their pilgrimage, Brahmans with red marks like seals on their foreheads, and others with the triple pronged fork-like mark of Siva in white and red. The men wore their hair long like women, sometimes done up in ample knots at the back of the head, and sometimes hanging down the back. All wore a sort of tight cotton skirt or piece of drapery checquered or patterned in colour wrapped round the loins, and depending from the waist to the feet; a white loose jacket frequently surmounted this, so that judging only from the back view, the stranger with European prepossessions as to dress distinctions between the sexes, might have some difficulty in saying which was which, or who was who, especially as the native women frequently wore similar skirts, white bodices, and their hair in knots. It was chiefly the beards that betrayed the gentlemen; otherwise the equality of the sexes was fairly well established, as to outward appearance at least, in the way that might astonish some of our Western reformers. It is true some of the men, like the ancient Egyptians, wore nothing above the skirt, except perhaps a white scarf on the shoulders, and the field-workers and coolies all down the Coromandel coast wore nothing but white turbans and waist cloths.

We passed the Silver Lake, really an inlet of the sea nearly surrounded by hills, the train startling large flocks of brown geese from the margin as it passed. Our old friends the white cranes we saw again lower down the line among the marshy pools. Paddy fields in various stages, often under water,

LADIES OR GENTLEMEN? (FASHIONS IN SOUTHERN INDIA)

irrigation wells drawn by oxen, as well as another pattern—like the Hungarian or Egyptian, a walking beam weighted at one end, the other having a rope attached to the bucket. The Southern Indian ones are, however, worked by the natives, generally two, working up and down from the centre, from which the beam swings, making it dip and rise again with bucket, the men steadying themselves by upright bamboos fixed each side, sometimes chanting a song to mark the time and enable them to move together.

Groves of palms were passed and pyramidal hills, bringing the same suggestion of Egypt we had had before, on the way to Chitorgarh. There was no doubt about getting further south as the temperature was much higher, the thermometer registering 75° to 80° and this was February 4, whereas only two days before we had been shivering over a fire at Darjeeling! In the burning sun we could see the dark figures in white turbans and waist cloths, coolies on the railway line, and ploughmen in the fields toiling in the heat. We stopped for breakfast at Berhampore. In the district from here to Vizianagram there was formerly a flourishing silk weaving industry among the natives. "All gone now," said a bright-looking European official in white drill and topi who entered our compartment. From what he told us further, it seems that this industry declined for very obvious causes—because the raw silk, the very material upon which it subsisted, was exported and consequently the occupation of the native handloom weavers was gone.

At Waltair, one passenger left, but our compartment was kept full as another immediately succeeded him and all four berths were occupied on the second night. One got more or less broken sleep, but perhaps more than might be expected.

At Bapatia next morning there was chota hazri, or early tea, ready, and it was very welcome. At Bitragunta there was a halt for breakfast. As we approached Madras, late in the afternoon, we came by lovely groves of palms, quite dark thick forests of them, with pools of water among them in which water lilies bloomed. Green parroquets decorated the telegraph wires, sitting in rows much as the swallows do in England in the autumn. The telegraph wires all over India are however a favourite resting perch with a variety of birds, and quick an observer may get a good notion of the variety of species in Indian Ornithology by noticing the many kinds of birds which may be seen in such positions, clearly silhouetted against the sky.

We arrived at the Beach Station, Madras, about five o'clock on February 4, relieved to have reached the end of our long journey. Hotel touts here may be described as active and strong on the wing. We eventually squeezed ourselves into a tickagary with our light baggage, and in spite of the presence of Moonsawmy—or perhaps in colusion with him—an officious native guide mounted the box and offered us information as to the public buildings we passed on the way to the hotel. The Prince of Wales's was full, but the proprietor advised us of another not far off, known as the Castle, which had formerly been the pavilion or palace of a native prince, and was a large two-storied yellow washed building with colonnades on the ground floor, and extensive terraces on to which the rooms opened out, on the first floor. These terraces were protected by a parapet which took the form of low battlements, whence possibly the hotel derived its name. There was a pleasant garden shaded by trees around the building, walled in from the road, and having entrance gates. Here we found agreeable rooms and plenty of space, without oppressive luxury or comfort, and as cool as might be expected, if it is ever cool anywhere in Madras? The hotel was under English management, and photographs of familiar places at Torquay and on the Cornish coast hung in our salon. Mosquito curtains told their usual tale, being generally a necessity in India, but are more particularly so at Madras.

On the drive from the station we passed Fort St George which dates from 1680, and is the only building of any historic interest. There were big Law Courts in a pretentious Italian Gothic style after the manner of modern Bombay architecture. The British traders and their stores and posters were in evidence, and "summer sales" going strong at the drapers, attracting smartly dressed English ladies in their motors and dog-carts. The streets were broad, and there was plenty of space everywhere. The hotels and bungalows were surrounded by large gardens, and abundant trees—palms being very plentiful.

It was pleasant to hear the clear notes of birds in the early morning, and of course we had the usual kite and crow chorus. In the evening there was a children's party going on at a pavilion in the garden, and popular European waltz tunes came from a piano.

The temperature in our rooms ranged from 75° to 80° and we felt anything but energetic. We had, moreover, in the afternoon an interesting drive out to the Adyar Library, the headquarters of the Theosophical Society built by Colonel Alcott who was now lying ill there. Having had a telegram from Mrs Annie Besant in the morning, a visit was arranged. She could not leave the Colonel, as he was then in a dying state. Our road lay between beautiful groves of palms of various kinds, mostly cocoa palms, and native villages, the huts of one story, long and low, and roofed with ridge tiles of a delightful bronze colour, the tiles, probably sun-baked, being doubled and trebled over and under alternately. The roads were covered with a fine dust of a rich reddish-brown tint, almost coffee colour, and this tint varied with the full red and bright white of the dresses of the natives, and their dark skins, and relieved by the clear light green of the paddy fields, and the gold and green of the palms, in the warm evening sunlight, made a fine harmony.

We passed a Hindu temple and a tank, and crossed a bridge over the broad river (Adyar) and on the other side presently drove under an ancient fragment of a stone carved gateway, and so through the wooded grounds to the Adyar Library, a new building of red brick and red sandstone of semi-Hindu type.

A lady clad in white conducted me to a large upper chamber very lofty and long in proportion to its width, furnished more or less like a European drawing-room, with chairs and couches, but high on the wall at intervals were various religious symbols, in white plaster relief, among which I noticed the Gammadion and the Serpent and the Tree. There was a pretty view over the river from the windows, on the side.

Presently Mrs Besant entered. She was robed in white. It was the sari dress of the native women in some fine soft material, with embroidered borders also white. Her hair too had whitened since I knew her in London many years before. We spoke of the old days—of Cunninghame Graham, G. Bernard Shaw, and Sidney Webb. Mrs Besant, once an active and ardent socialist, seemed to have quite removed herself into another world, strikingly different from the one of strife and protest in which she with her wonderful eloquence had been a potent influence, and was now devoting her life to inculcating the principles of Theosophy and educational work among the young Hindus. Her idea was to gather the best elements out of all religions, and to unite them in one comprehensive creed, the keynote of which, as I understood, is universal brotherhood. In her schools she desired to cultivate the higher side of the native Hindu religion, refining and spiritualising, though by no means Europeanizing, but preserving all native characteristics in dress and courteous manners, and as far as possible preventing any Western contamination.

In the great hall on the ground floor the first thing that catches the visitor's eye is the text inscribed aloft on the entablature in large carved characters—" There is no religion higher than truth."

On the walls of this hall, also, are carved in stone another series of symbols, treated as a series of panels in relief, and among these it was interesting to find Mr Holman Hunt's well-known picture "The Light of the World," reproduced in relief by a native sculptor. In a recess in the opposite wall was a life-size seated portrait of Madame Blavatsky in marble. It was intended to place a statue of Colonel Alcott standing beside her, Mr Besant told me. His loss will be a severe one for the Society.

We drove back by way of the Triplicane or Mohammedan quarter—the native bazaar, a brilliant scene of colour and movement. On the way we passed several "Toddy Tappers," as they are called, at work on the palm and stems. These are natives who extract a sort of spirit from the palm, and who, clad only in white turbans and waist-cloths, climb the tall, smooth columnar stems of the cocoa palm, by a curious method—a sort of loop of cane which encircles the upper part of the body, and hooks round the tree stem. This they shift in jerks as they climb, using their legs and feet in the usual way as a grip on the stem. We noticed the small, gourd-like bottles attached to some of the trees, which are placed so as to catch the juice from incisions made in the bark. The spirit made from this juice is sold in the bazaars.

The jin-rickshaw is much in use in Madras as a means of locomotion, and some of them will even carry two people at once, though this seems heavy for one boy. The native boys who draw them are, however, active enough and but little encumbered with clothes, and are always eager

MADRAS—A JIN-RICKSHAW MADE FOR TWO

for custom. Mount Road in the main thoroughfare in the European quarter, and here all the principal shops and stores are situated. These as buildings were mostly pretentious and tasteless. St George's cathedral was a semi-classic church with a pointed spire. The Post Office had red-tiled gabled spires of a more or less Swiss type, with iron crestings, and arcaded balconies on each story. One sees relics of eighteenth century semi-classic taste in some of the older houses with plastered walls yellow and white-washed. The vast gardens which broke the continuity of the buildings, and often isolated them, and the pleasant avenue-like character of the main roads, always lined with shady trees, made up for many architectural short-comings, and again suggested spacious ideas for a garden city.

At the head of Mount Road was the Munro statue where other roads diverged—a bronze statue by Chantry of a gentleman in a cloak pointing—probably to indicate his line of policy, though, more literally, he might be taken to be showing the stranger what a long way he was from Madras. The electric trams are no doubt useful as the distances are enormous and dusty, walking being impossible for Europeans, as they would soon be covered with a powdering of fine red dust.

We paid a visit one evening to the Botanic Gardens where we saw the Victoria Regia (which is usually associated with the inside of a hot-house at Kew) growing in the open on a lake. There were beautiful palms here and many varieties of trees. One we noted was covered with white blossoms which looked and smelled like orange or lemon flowers, and had green fruit of an egg shape, hanging from its branches.

Madras we found too oppressive and inervating to stay long, and so on February 8th we departed for Tanjore, rising at 4.30 A.M. to catch an early train, and were only able to snatch a hasty hazri, and get into a belated carriage and drive through the gloom of the early morning—or rather by the dim light of the waning moon to the station for the 5.45 train South.

Our compartment was shared at different stages of the journey by British officers. A Babu with a quantity of baggage, and three German Mission people—a gentleman and two ladies with still more baggage,. who filled it pretty well up to Tanjore.

The country seemed very productive, and on each side of the line most of the way were large crops of paddy, much of it under water. In many places, too, the natives were ploughing *in* the water. The crops in some of the fields (or rather pastures separated by low banks of earth) were a brilliant light green, in others the grain was ripe, and was being reaped with hooks by the natives, while further on they would be threshing and stacking the straw. The method of threshing out the grain was primitive. A man would hold a loose sheaf in his hand and beat it hard, several times in succession, on the ground; this shook out the grain, and then he would cast the straw that remained to the men who were stacking it near by. They made low wide stacks straight on to the bare earth. The women gathered up the paddy as it was reaped.

We passed more fine groves of cocoa palms, distant hills were visible inland here and there, and there were generally large sheets of water each side of the line, but the rivers which we frequently crossed were almost dry.

The crowds of natives at all the stations were

again very interesting. The men generally wearing their hair long and done up in knots. In fact the men had finer and more luxuriant heads of hair than the women, whose hair was usually short and fuzzy. Sometimes the men had their foreheads and temples shaved, and let their hair grow freely at the back. Caste marks were painted very boldly and distinctly on the dark foreheads. The sacred mark of Siva occurring most frequently—a red vertical stroke in the centre between two white lines radiating from the nose.

The men also wore the coloured skirt tightly wrapped about their middle and falling to their feet, the upper parts of their bodies being left bare, except for a loose white scarf, like a towel, thrown over their shoulders. The coolies and agriculturists wore nothing but turbans and waist-cloths. The women invariably wore silver nose rings, earings and anklets, and the Sari dress. Mahomedans seemed to be very scarce in these parts. As to colour, reds and whites prevailed in the dresses. Sometimes the vivid crude (magenta) aniline pink which has become unfortunately too common in India was to be seen. A favourite blend was red and yellow in the women's Sari dresses, in stripes, or crossed tartan-wise.

Light cakes, bananas, and painted toys and other trifles were hawked about at the stations, the sellers uttering curious cries and chants. Every station had its tap of water, and always a thirsty throng of natives from their crowded compartments would be seen clustering around it filling their bright brass drinking cups, which they invariably carry, quenching their thirst and washing themselves.

Apropos of the refreshment stations, I find a note in my journal as to what appears to have been a particularly unsatisfactory Tiffin at Villuparam, for which we were induced to pay 1 rupee 8 annas in advance, but of which "only a little currie was really eatable." How much more sensible (perchance not so profitable) it would be to give travellers the chance of ordering from the carte, and paying according to a fixed tariff. Travellers are by no means always able to eat the provided meal, and need milk and easily digestible foods, and simple cookery. The hard meat, stringy fowl, and messed up dishes usually offered are very inappropriate, if not positively injurious food. Simply cooked sound fresh food is a great want at hotels and railway stations all over India.

We arrived at Tanjore between 6 and 7 in the evening. There were sleeping and refreshment rooms at the station. The station-master met us and said that a room would be vacant at 9 o'clock, as Lord and Lady ——? who then occupied them were leaving by the 9 P.M. mail. In the meantime we had a ladies' waiting-room to ourselves and could dine during the interval. The sleeping rooms were across a bridge on the other side of the line in a new terraced building, with an English housekeeper sort of woman to receive us and our rupees. There was quite an up-to-date porcelain bath, but, on examination, one tap was cut off, and there was no water in the other! There were spring beds and mosquito curtains, and it was a fairly cool room.

TANJORE—THE GREAT GATE OF THE TEMPLE

The system here was to charge 1 rupee 8 annas for a room for the first twelve hours, and if occupied for longer then the rate was higher.

Hearing there was a good Dak bungalow near by, we decided to take up our quarters there the next morning and found it quite nice, cool, quiet, old-fashioned and unpretentious, and their being no other travellers we had it all to ourselves. From what the native in charge said it appeared that the new station rooms rather injured his custom, as travellers now mostly stayed there.

Our exploration of Tanjore commenced by driving to the Old Fort within which stands the great Hindu Temple dedicated to Siva. The great gateway is approached by a bridge over a moat, then dry, which surrounds the Fort. The outer gate is plastered and is crowned by a row of figures of deities in niches which are brightly coloured. The great gateway is of yellow sandstone and is richly carved—a mass of figures and detail. The image of the god Siva and his various incarnations constantly appears. Various legends connected with these are painted on the walls of the court at the back of an arcade, and are exceedingly curious.

The great Nandi, or sacred Bull of Siva, a colossal image of a recumbent Bull, richly ornamented with chains and bells around his neck, is seen on a pedestal approached by steps in the centre of the court, under a pillared and decorated canopy. When we saw it first a magnificent peacock had perched himself upon the head of the bull, his tail drooping over its neck. The bull was carved out of a fine black stone, really syenite, but much darkened by libations of oil with which the image is constantly anointed. It has all the character of the type of zebu in this district. We saw its living prototype in a street of Tanjore—a splendid black bull (short-horned) lying down with its yoke companion, a white one, equally noble looking.

The pillared front of the small temple close by was richly coloured, and on a sort of frieze was a series of portraits of the reigning family of Maharajahs.

The Temple guide spoke a little English, but occasionally would stop for want of words, but we generally gathered his meaning, and he seemed unusually intelligent.

Ganesha, the elephant god (of generation) frequently appeared among the others, Siva and Parvati being the chief. One of the scenes painted on the wall of the arcade, already spoken of, represented the wedding of Siva and Parvati, who stood, hand in hand, with a tree in the middle —like Adam and Eve. Among the guests at this wedding were represented two giants, one whose appetite seemed to know no limit, while the thirst of the other was unquenchable. The first was shown devouring all kinds of food, and to express the drinking capacity of the other a stream of water full of fish was flowing into the mouth of the other. These were very primitive paintings, but expressive. The figures were drawn in black outline and filled in with flat tints. At the gate of the Temple there were drawings on the white-washed wall in thick outline in Indian red, in quite a different style and no doubt of a much later date. A large number of

Lingams were shown in rows placed together in one corner of the court, and there were many Lingam shrines in the arcade besides. Here and there was colouring on the carved figures, but, as a rule, the elaborately carved pagodas were left in yellow sandstone, which had blackened where exposed to the weather, and it may have been that colour had been worn off.

The later temple (dating from about the fifteenth century) had remarkably delicate carving on its lower courses, the edges being frequently pierced. At the steps of the entrance an elephant, carved on each side, formed the balustrade, each having two trunks, one curling inwards and holding a man in its coil, and the second extended and terminating in a volute at the end of the steps on each side.

There was a noticeable point, as giving further evidence of primitive wooden construction, in the carved detail under the eaves of the great temple where there was a sort of intersected lattice work faithfully rendered in stone. It recalled the screens of bamboo and matting, commonly used in this district, added on to the edges of the tiled roofs in front of the huts and bungalows as extra shields from the sun, and this carved stone lattice work may have been derived from the wood work and the cane and wicker structure of the primitive buildings which preceded the use of stone.

In the court of the great temple, in a shed (roofed with corrugated iron I regret to say), we saw the cars used for the procession through the city, on the occasion of the great annual festival in March, which appears to be similar to the Juggernaut.

The high pyramidal canopied roof, supported on columns, was carved like the pagoda of a temple, which, in fact, it represented. The image of the god being placed within. The car would be drawn by a pair of oxen.

We saw afterwards a religious procession of the kind passing down the principal street. Two men carried a banner in front, a piece of red cloth suspended between two poles. After them came a band playing tom-toms and hautboys, such as we heard at Benares. Then came the car drawn by two zebus, with its high pagoda, accompanied by priests in white robes, with long hair and marks on their foreheads.

It struck me as remarkable how closely the dress of the native men here resembles that of the people of ancient Egypt as pictured on the monuments. Indeed, the Hindu pantheon itself suggests a certain kinship to the symbolic Egyptian religion, embracing, as it appears to do, the deification of all natural forces and types of animals and birds. The Hindus have their elephant god, their monkey god, and their parrot god, for instance, each figured with the animal's head but otherwise human, just as the Egyptians imaged their hawk-headed, cat-headed, and other deities. The ox of Osiris, too, seems to present a parallel to the sacred bull of Siva.

We next visited the tank in the citadel, noted for the purity of its water, but it looked muddy enough we thought, and felt no inclination to test the sample offered us by a native in a cup.

Near the tank was a very plain Christian church, dating from about the end of the 18th century or the beginning of the 19th, absolutely bare of ornament or symbol, with the exception of a small mural monument at the west end—a bas-relief in marble by Flaxman, in memory of one Schwartz, a British missionary. Not, however, a very good specimen of the sculptor's work, and looking as if it had been rather done to order, and though it had Flaxman's characteristic broad simple treatment, was rather over smooth and "goody-goody" in expression—a missionary looking benevolent on his death-bed, clerical attendant and probable successor at his side, group of good boys in front, and row of turbaned Indians, presumably converts, on the other side of the bed.

It was curious to see this bare, gaunt, puritanical-looking church, planted almost in the shadow of the great Hindu temple with its frank nature worship, pantheism, and riot of symbolism and imagery.

From the citadel and the temples we drove over the bridge across the river into the city to see the palace of the Maharajah. Not a very beautiful building — a big, rambling, yellow-washed pile, looking rather untidy and neglected. In the guard-room at the entrance gate, there was a portrait of the father of the present prince. Through a corridor, the walls of which were painted with quaint figures, we reached a small chamber, open on one side, but painted on the three other walls with large equestrian portraits of three Maharajahs—grandfather, father, and son. They were in profile, very richly dressed, and on finely caparisoned horses, with hunting dogs—the dogs running underneath the horses. These mural portraits were painted in tempers, apparently, on the white-washed wall, and had flaked off in places, but they were good characteristic Indian work, and reminded one a little in treatment of European mediæval design, such as may be seen in Burgundian tapestries of the end of the fifteenth century.

We next came to a small court where we saw the Durbar Hall, divided from the court by an open colonnade. Inside was a miscellaneous collection of objects—portraits, rather dreary ones of the Maharajahs and favourite hounds, some on very dilapidated canvasses with holes through them—old fashioned French lithographs of the early "fifties," much fly-blown; a handsome palanquin, with dragons' heads on the ends of the poles; another one was carved, and plated with ivory. There was also a beautiful ivory fan, of a large size and peculiar shape, probably to be used as a punka. Then, too, there was a bronze bust of Lord Nelson, presented by some English lady to a former Maharajah, and her own work. Then we saw the library, which contained quite a large collection of old-fashioned English books—in eighteenth and early nineteenth century bindings—such as a set of *The Spectator*, Hayley's Poems, Burns, Scott, etc., and also an extensive library of Hindu and Tamil manuscripts. These were peculiar in form, and consisted of long oblong sheets of a roughish sort of paper, rather resembling papyrus in quality, protected by thin boards on loose covers of thin wood, secured round the middle by ties. These covers were sometimes lacquered on their outsides in various designs. On one I noticed the typical design representing Vishnu, with the lotus flower springing from his navel which contains the figure of Buddha, Laksmi looking on in wonder. These figures were drawn in black outline on gold, the gold high-toned with coloured lacquers. A smell of naphtha or some such moth antidote pervaded the place.

We were then shown the armoury, where there were some rather showy sporting guns of English make, bearing the name of Mortimer & Co., and elaborately chased. There were very vile portraits of King Edward VII. and Queen Alexandra.

After this we saw another Durbar Hall—the Maharana's—adorned with more dreary portraits of the family and a few stuffed birds. The most curious thing was a real skeleton in a real cupboard, side by side with a skeleton beautifully imitated in ivory. There they hung inside a plain upright cupboard, looking like a hanging wardrobe—but what a wardrobe! What hung there needed no robes!

Down the main street of Tanjore there were placed at intervals very curious and richly carved wooden pagodas, apparently very old, upon cars with massive wheels of wood, somewhat like rude ox-cart wheels, some of them being discs. These were probably used in processions at the festivals.

The houses were generally low, and of only one story, with the low-pitched ridge-tiled roofs as at Madras, the porches and raised terraces on platforms in front forming the shops, being further protected from the sun by lean-to extra roofs or screens of matting and bamboo, sometimes supported on uprights of cocoa palm stems. Occasionally these screens are supported by growing trees which spread their foliage above. Pumpkins and gourds are often grown upon the tiled roofs, and have a charming effect with their wandering stems, green leaves, and golden spheres of fruit scattered over the rich brown tiles.

The roads are deep in red-brown dust as at Madras, and there is a continual traffic of little covered tongas drawn by little trotting zebus in single harness. We had a broken-down victoria to drive in, and a fearful old crock of a horse, given to jibbing and really not fit to drive. The carriage seats were sliding ones, too!

Tanjore spreads itself over a large area of open spaces, interspersed with trees, gardens, and tanks. The water is abundant, and washing operations frequent. There is no coherent plan about the town, the streets wandering about into open space, and leaving off in a casual sort of way. There was a considerable market going on in provisions, and there was a silk-weaving quarter where may be seen the native weavers stretching long threads of silk on bamboo frames the whole length of the street, and winding it off on to wheels—our carriage nearly collided with one in a narrow street. The raw silk is often wound round short staves.

We visited a weaver's shop, and were shown some hand-woven silk saris, brocaded with silver thread, the silver being turned into gold by some colouring process. A dress of ten yards can be bought of this beautiful material for 24 rupees.

Red and purple are the principal colours, and these, with the gold thread woven in border designs of elephants, horses and peacocks, have a very gorgeous effect.

European influence seems to have declined in Tanjore, although there are numerous Christian missions about. What strikes the unprejudiced spectator is the extreme unsuitability of any modern western type of Protestant Christianity, with all that it involves to the native mind, to say nothing of climate and habit.

Western influence, it is true, asserts itself to the eye, at least, in the form of an ugly clock tower, and we passed "The Tanjore Union Club," where we saw native gentlemen in their cool, white, loose clothing playing lawn tennis in a well laid-out court. But the life of the mass of the people goes on unchanged as it has done for ages.

In driving through the town we saw many little white-washed temples among the native houses their richly-carved pagodas rising above the low brown tiled roofs. At the doors are quaint paintings of elephants or tigers, and the white walls of the shops and dwellings are frequently ornamented in the same way with curious figures, among which occurs not unfrequently the English soldier with a dragoon's helmet and jack-boots. Outside a liquor shop I saw, painted rather boldly in red outline, a European lady and gentleman refreshing themselves with wine-glasses in their hands. The lady's costume reproduced the rather fussy fashion of twenty-five or thirty years ago, the frills and furbelows quite carefully worked out with the

Indian love of detail, but somehow the general effect was rather Elizabethan than Victorian.

In passing along one of the streets we heard a sound of tom-toms, and presently saw approaching on a zebu cart a large theatrical poster painted on the outer sides of two large boards leaning together, tent-wise, on the cart. These bore announcements in Hindustani and Arabic, with pictures of exciting scenes — Rajahs flourishing scimitars over people, and so forth. Natives walked alongside the cart distributing pink bills of the performances printed in Arabic, while the tom-toms attracted attention to the forthcoming show.

In the evening we drove to the theatre, accompanied by our bearer. We reached an open ground outside the town; it was rather dark, but we saw a row of lights in front of us, and heard the sound of tom-toms. The old horse jibbed and would not go further, so we left the carriage, and Moonsawmy conducted us to some temporary structures of matting and bamboo, where tickets were sold. One rupee secured a chair in the front row. The theatre was a large, tent-like structure, with plastered piers supporting a roof of matting. The floor was of earth, the common ground, in fact, upon which the back rows squatted. The stage was also of earth, raised about three or four feet, the front being painted in broad red and white vertical stripes. The footlights were ordinary oil lamps, clustered in groups. The audience was entirely native (besides ourselves, who were the only Europeans present). Some sat close up alongside the stage on raised steps of earth. Dark draperies hung at the sides of the proscenium, and there was a coarsely-painted drop scene, of the kind

TANJORE—NATIVE THEATRE—HOUSE FULL. PERFORMANCE FROM 9 P.M. TILL 2 A.M.—BUT WE DIDN'T STOP TO SEE IT THROUGH

familiar in third-rate provincial theatres and music-halls at home.

The first scene apparently represented a suburban street in the European quarter of an Indian town; at least there was a square towered church in it, ugly enough, although some high-pitched gables rather suggested suburban England. A road in very acute perspective ran through the centre of the scene, which might, after all, have been bought from some European travelling theatre.

The curtain raiser was of a sort of operatic, conventional courtship motive, and consisted of a musical dialogue between a young lady and gentleman of uncertain country, costume, and period. The girl was badly dressed in a white muslin frock, with a little red silk waistband, and a tinsel coronet or tiara on her head. She kept her eyes on the ground the whole time, and moved stiffly and shyly; her action, as well as that of the gentleman, being rather suggestive of marionettes.

The lady began by singing, each strophe or couplet being repeated or answered by an antistrophe from a chorus concealed behind the scenes, to the accompaniment of tom-toms. The little wooer presently appeared (also a girl), dressed in a cap of tinsel, a tunic of black velvet trimmed with silver tinsel, and breeches of the same, with brown hose or boots. He also began singing strophes, which were responded to or repeated by the chorus, and the lady replied in the same way. Whenever the lover made any advances the lady repelled them, and, after each of her sung speeches, crossed over to the opposite side of the stage, the lover doing the same. After a long course of this monotonous question and answer, sing-song business, they finally came to terms, and stood singing together, the lover with his arm round the lady's shoulders. A harmonium, playing at the wings, assisted the tom-toms.

The *pièce de resistance* next began. The first scene was a room of state in a Rajah's palace. The Rajah and his grand vizier, and an old priest or soothsayer in a turban and Indian dress, were the characters. The Rajah was a white man, of a rather Irish cast of countenance. He was dressed in black and silver, having wonderful silver spangles in circular patches as big as dinner plates down the front of his trousers. He wore a sabre at his side, and he was seated on a throne mounted on several steps, and each step was decorated by a large globe of silvered Bohemian glass. The vizier was attired in a similar way, but not quite so gorgeous as the king.

From our bearer's interpretation it appeared that the Rajah, or king, who commenced chanting in a most doleful and monotonous way, was in trouble for want of an heir to the throne, and consulted the turbaned old gentleman about it, who gave his advice at considerable length.

The next scene showed the interior of a temple; an image of the sacred bull was there, and a black man, clad only in a waist cloth, was officiating, apparently as priest. He was also evidently regarded as a comic actor by the audience, and it was rather curious to observe that his obvious burlesque of some native religious observances were received with laughter. He seemed to put the Rajah, the vizier, and the soothsayer, who now entered, through their religious paces, waving a brush over them and putting garlands round their necks, uttering curious gibberish the while, with extravagant action, which seemed vastly to amuse the audience.

The next scene showed the Rajah seated again in his palace, and to him entered a troop of zenanas to announce the joyful news of the birth of an heir; but after they had departed with many salaams, something seemed to go wrong, and the Rajah began his doleful plaint again. The soothsayer and the vizier were again consulted, and both had a good deal to say, but matters did not seem to mend much, and the scene promising to be interminably long, we felt we had had about as much of the drama as we could do with, and hearing, moreover, that the performance would continue until 2 A.M., having commenced at nine, we left Moonsawmy to sit it out, after he had found us our carriage.

The next day we had another drive through the city and its surroundings, reaching a pleasant region of palm-groves, and lakes where buffaloes were enjoying a bath. They lie in the water quite deeply, with often only their heads out or the ridges of their backs showing.

At the bungalow various native pedlars and travelling merchants came up with their bundles, and, as we sat under the verandah, they would untie these and spread out their wares before us. These were generally new silver and copper repoussé dishes and bowls, samples of the craft of the Tanjore district, but not good, being vulgar and mechanical in workmanship, although repeating traditional patterns and representations of the chief deities of the Hindu pantheon. Some of these were embossed in silver, or rather were partly silvered over the copper, leaving bright copper in parts, but they had rather a flashy and tasteless appearance. The best things were the small antique bronzes and brass objects—bulls, horses, birds, peacocks, lamps, and curious shaped vessels, and many of these were highly interesting. A pair of bronze stirrups I acquired were charmingly designed, and showed delicate design and workmanship.

In the town they make a kind of brass standard lamp, in various sizes, having a moulded stem supporting a shallow vessel for the oil, with niches from four inches, the brass image of a cock is usually placed at the top as a sort of finial. The parts are made to unscrew like the well-known antique Roman lamp which, in general design and structure, this Tanjore lamp strongly recalled. Some, indeed, were terminated by ring handles just like the Roman ones.

We had been fairly comfortable at the Dak bungalow, and the two brothers who kept it were most anxious to please. The cooking was unusually good, and the place was certainly very quiet. The windows had no glass, but were closed with Venetian shutters (which did not always act, however, satisfactorily). The floors were covered with India matting, and the beds were furnished with mosquito nets. The meals were nicely served, and the table always decked with flowers. The thermometer in our rooms registered usually about 75 degrees, whereas at Madras it went up to 80 degrees.

Water was not carried here in goat-skins as in Bombay and the North-West and Central Provinces, but in large earthen jars. A man would carry one in each hand, or slung by strings from a stick over the shoulder. There was a fine young native who watered the garden in front of our bungalow—he had a splendid figure, and was almost the colour of ebony. I tried to get hold of him to get a study from him, but somehow he was not to be found when the time came, and another very inferior specimen was offered in his stead.

We left Tanjore on the evening of February 11 for Trichinopoly. It is only a two hours' journey by the railway, and we arrived quite punctually about 8.30. It was too dark to see much of the country, or get anything but a vague idea of the place, especially when under the cover of an ox tonga, two of which vehicles conveyed us and our baggage to the travellers' bungalow about a mile off, the little zebus trotting along at a brisk pace as fast as ponies, and much better conditioned than any tonga ponies we saw in India.

At the bungalow we found an English lady and gentleman, a newly arrived official and his wife, who had not yet got a house—who were then dining by candle light on the verandah—in possession of the best room, and had to make the best of it in a small side room, poorly furnished, and with no mosquito nets. We got some soda and milk and turned in, but, alas, the beds were hard as nails and the mosquitoes troublesome and strong on the wing, while the temperature went up to 80 degrees again!

After breakfast the next morning we got a carriage (which was a considerable improvement both as to vehicle and horse to the one at Tanjore), and

TRICHINOPOLY—OX TONGA—VITA BREVIS!

drove towards the fort, which stands conspicuously on a bold rock rising abruptly from the plain. Passing through the native bazaar we crossed over a long bridge, which spanned a very broad river thronged with bathers, and people washing clothes, and watering cattle, all busy in the stream which was quite shallow, not more than waist high. This bridge had been designed and built by an English engineer, somewhere in the forties. It was of red sandstone, and our driver pointed out a stone in the coping inscribed to certain English officers who served under Clive, and helped to lay "the foundations of the British Empire in India" in 1750-4.

At about two miles from Trichinopoly we came to the great Temple of Seringham. Thatched native huts, forming a sort of bazaar, led up to and were clustered about the great gates, which resembled the entrance to the Temple of Tanjore. The height of the gateways were very great in proportion to their width. The great pagodas piled over them were carved with the greatest richness and intricacy of detail, and covered with the figures of gods and imagery of all kinds, surmounted by the curious rounded long barrel-like cresting, which is so characteristic of Hindu temple-architecture. The sculptured or modelled work here was all coloured, but many of the figures were said to be in stucco.

I think we passed through three of these gateways before we reached the final one leading into the court, with a many columned pavilion in the centre, having a painted ceiling in which the Hindu gods figured. The great Temple of Seringham is sacred to Vishnu, whose image appears very frequently. Opposite to this central pavilion is a colonnade having a frieze of carved and coloured figures under a cresting, Vishnu being in the centre. This seemed to be the Hindu equivalent for a sculptured pediment. The effect of the thickly clustered columns of white-washed stone supporting this band of rich carving and colour was very striking, the sharp light and shade of noontide throwing the front into strong relief, and through the aisles formed by the columns we could see another lighted court beyond.

The main passage through was lined by the little stalls of a bazaar, grouped at the bases of the columns, where mementoes in the shape of small tin pictures heightened with coloured lacquer were stamped in relief with representations of Vishnu and his goddess, bead rosaries and necklaces, and jewellery were also sold, and little silk bags embroidered with portraits of the same deities.

As we stood facing the second court, the sacred elephant of the temple came up, his forehead bearing the mark of Vishnu, painted large in red and white. It was amusing to see the animal pick up a two-anna piece from the ground, and pass it over its head to its keeper and driver seated on its neck. Another younger and smaller elephant soon joined the other, and this one had beautiful tusks which his larger companion was without. This one, too, skilfully picked up the small coins in the same way, fumbling with the sensitive finger-like point of his trunk to get hold of them in the crannies of the pavement.

We then, passing across this second court, entered the Hall of a Thousand Columns—a sort of architectural forest. Before this is reached, however, there is a smaller hall which has a very remarkable range of carved columns—the most extraordinary carved stone work in Southern India. They are strictly speaking rather columnar brackets, bracketed columns or corbels resting on bases, and they represent warriors on horses spearing lions and tigers.. The chief feature in each is the rearing

THE SACRED ELEPHANTS OF SERINGHAM—SECURING TWO-ANNA PIECES!

horse, which with its rider and lance, and smaller figures below, and the attacking tiger, or, sometimes, elephant, form a connected group cut out of a single block of stone. These sculptures have so barbaric and antique an appearance that it seems surprising they should only date from the seventeenth and eighteenth centuries together with the whole of the temple buildings.

A curious effect is given to the interior of some of the temples here by the practice of whitewashing the pillars and walls, and leaving the carved figures untouched in the stone, which gives them by contrast an unusually swarthy appearance.

Returning, we had a view of the Rock of Trichinopoly with the old fort and temple on the summit. This syenite rock crops out in various places in this district, but not often rising much above the ground, but only emerging here and there from the earth in a manner rather suggestive of the backs of tortoises.

Saw a mongoose at the roadside which soon crept out of sight and hid in the low brushwood at our approach. Trichinopoly is well wooded, but is not particularly picturesque, though the scattered tiled or thatched bungalows look pretty enough in their gardens, but on the whole it gives one the impression of rather a straggling place. There was a deserted looking mission church with a few tombstones about it quite near our bungalow, trying to look like an English village church, but not succeeding. Leipzig Lutherans and Wesleyan Methodists are said to have "missions" here, as well as the Church of England. These missionaries seem to plant their stations wherever there are important Hindu temples. The wonder is that the natives are so tolerant.

Madura was our next destination, and we were not sorry to get away from our stifling little barn of a room at the bungalow, leaving in the early morning about daybreak for the 5.45 Madras mail.

The country was flat at first, with, again, large sheets of water along the sides of the line, but as we passed from the Trichinopoly district to the Madura district we entered a mountainous region, thickly wooded. I noted many cedar trees, and a kind of cactus growing high with tall tree-like stem. It was an interesting and varied country the rest of the way. The crops were chiefly paddy and castor oil plant.

One station had the extraordinary name of Ammayanayakanur, and we were soon in the tobacco-growing district, passing Dindigul with a rock and an old fort upon it, not unlike Trichinopoly in character. Cigars of the district were offered at the station, but we saw no tobacco crops near the line.

We reached Madura about noon, in time for tiffin, and engaged a room at the station, which was a great improvement as to beds and general appointments on our recent bungalow experiences. The sleeping-rooms were built out on a separate wing which appeared to be new. They opened on to a corridor which led to a large open terrace, and were in charge of a Eurasian woman. There was also a good dining-room at the station.

It was tremendously hot, however, and we could not very well move out until after 4 o'clock, when having engaged a guide we drove out to see the great temple. Our bearer objected strongly to the guide and there was some friction between them, but as native servants were prohibited from entering the temples, and were always stopped at the

THE RIVALS. OUR MOONSAWMY AND THE MADURA GUIDE

gates, Moonsawmy could not show cause why the guide was not necessary, and we found him very intelligent, speaking English well, and having the history of the place at his fingers' ends.

The Madura temple is so remarkable and is on such a scale that I was anxious to get all the information about it I could. Mr Pillai (the guide) was very useful and well-informed, and he gave us many interesting stories and details about the sculptured figures and paintings.

There are four great pagoda-gates, richly carved and painted, of the same type but larger than those at Tanjore and Trichinopoly. Evidently the Hindus had no scruples about colouring their sculpture, and the colouring has been renewed from time to time. The prevailing tints used are turquoise blue, vermilion, yellow, white, and green. One of the gates the guide pointed out was granite up to the first story, and the figures were in stucco above.

The four gates mentioned are connected by a high wall, on the crest of which occur at intervals the image of Siva (to whom the temple is dedicated) seated between two bulls, the bulls being placed upon the top of the wall, and the image of the God in a sort of arched recess, sunk into it a little below. The upper part of the wall is uncoloured, but a sort of high dado is carried along it below, painted in broad vertical stripes of red and white which seems a favourite scheme of decoration in Southern India. The wall encloses a broad paved court, and inside this is another wall with gates, through which the various temples and columned halls are entered.

In the centre of all is the sacred tank, a large pool of water surrounded by steps, and an arcade of white columns. As we approached this, we saw a crowd of natives, men and women, seated on the paved margin of the tank along one side and between the columns listening to a priest who was preaching with much earnestness. Our guide said he was translating or expounding (one did not know with what gloss) passages from the sanskrit text of the sacred books which another priest previously read in the original.

The scene was a picturesque one. The various colours of the people's dresses, in which dark red prevailed, showed against the white wall and columns, and the brown faces made a harmonious scheme of colour.

The wall along the upper part was painted with a series of histories of Siva and his incarnations. These picture-stories were arranged in tiers or friezes, about four or five deep, one above the other, and running the entire length of the wall behind the colonade, each side the tank. These paintings were highly interesting, painted probably with the main object of making the stories intelligible to the people, they were quite decorative, full of detail, and forming a rather closely filled and dark pattern of colour, having the effect of a woven hanging.

One of the painted legends treated of a certain Maharajah who appears to have persecuted the early Jain seceders, much as the Roman emperor treated the early Christians, with great ferocity, finally impaling them on stakes, and thus they were painted all of a row!

The Jain sect was at first apparently regarded as a schism, and the Jains as heretics or apostates falling away from the pure Hindu worship of Siva.

One seems here, in this great Temple of Madura, to get back to the most ancient type of religion, and one which, after all, allowing for evolution in our ideas, seems the most lasting—Nature worship. The Hindus in their pantheon include and embrace everything, at least in their own universe, which is their own country, and to them, truly, "nothing is common or unclean." Their deities incarnate themselves in all sorts of forms. Siva, according to one legend, for instance, even taking the form of a wild sow, and suckling the young of the mother which had been slain by the hunters. The second son of Siva rides upon a peacock, the representative bird of India. The Zebu bull is sacred to Siva, and in the Lingam is symbolised and revered the male and female principle of generation, the root and source of all life on the earth.

In one place in the temple, between two of the columns, was a group of the nine planets personified and placed around the sun—a golden sphere in the centre. For each of these embodied planets might be found a corresponding personality among the deities of the classical world.

Another striking thing about the Madura temple is the force of realization and expression in the figure sculpture. Life-sized figures of different gods and demons are carved in stone in front of the columns in many of the halls of the temple, the columns themselves frequently white-washed, while the figures are left in the untouched stone and look in contrast like bronze figures, their elaborate detail and undercutting emphasizing this suggestion. Indeed, the variety of character, invention, as well as the vigour and freedom, governed by a certain formalism, of some of this sculpture at its best reminds one of European gothic sculpture in the

Middle Ages, not only in its symbolical and legendary aspect, but also its all embracing character and sympathy with the life of the people. The type of the Hindu mother appears, for instance, in one of the best of the figures carrying her child on her hip, just as the native women do to this day, while a suckling infant is suspended at her breast.

Mockery, if not humour, too, seems to come out here and there sometimes, as in the dancing figure of a mocking musician playing on his pipes.

A frequent subject is Siva presenting his sister in marriage to Vishnu, and there are besides a number of curious legends connected with the sculptures here, which are very various, and, of course, not unfrequently become grotesque or monstrous under the influence of the Hindu religious symbolic ideas and the Hindu inventiveness; but one feels that here is a genuine piece of ancient life, expressed in the forms of Hindu art—frank nature worship in full vigour of life, and a dominant influence in the lives of millions of people.

In the sacred tank the people were constantly bathing and washing their clothes. The water never seems to be changed and is perfectly green in colour. Our guide said it remained pure and ordered a man to show its quality by dipping his hands in and holding a small quantity in them, cupwise. The water, however, was, even in this small quantity, quite green, although a clear green. It must have been full of vegetable matter, one would think. It reminded us of what the Maharajah's secretary had said of the Ganges water at Benares.

The colouring of the interior of the Temple in

parts recalled the mural decoration of ancient Egypt in its use of simple primary colours—red, green, white, and yellow prevailing. The lotus flower, too, was constantly introduced, treated as a rosette upon the ceilings.

Some of the pillared halls were, however, left in plain stonework, or simply whitewashed. One long hall we entered looked very impressive in the dim light, a single ray from the sun penetrating, and making a spot of intense light upon the floor.

We saw a gilded copper dome, and a golden flag staff, and our guide pointed out the great doors behind which the festival cars were kept, and we saw, too, wonderfully decorated life-sized images of elephants and horses which formed part of the show on great occasions. There were two black and two white elephants, standing between the columns, under rather tawdry and tinselly canopies, and other furniture of the festivals; one large hanging bearing the words of welcome to the Prince and Princess of Wales, which must have been used for the occasion of their visit.

Various donors of parts of the temple were pointed out, in effigy. The Czar of Russia appeared (not however in person) as the donor of certain shrines and a brass canopy or arch which held many lamps.

The practice of drawing the image of the god on festival days through the streets on great cars seems general at all the chief temples in Southern India, and not confined to Juggernath. At Seringham we saw the great car on which the image of Siva was drawn on such occasions, and also the thick

SACRED TANK OF THE GREAT TEMPLE, MADURA

cables—like ship's cables—which were used for the purpose—multitudes of men hauling the car out of the temple and along the streets by these means. Here, too, at Madura the god Siva is represented seated upon his car which is treated as a kind of throne, the wheels and the horses sculptured at the sides in a symbolic sort of way.

In some of the painted histories on the walls, Siva is shown in a winged car (suggesting his rapid flight and omnipresence, perhaps) and, presumably, his image is drawn out on a car at festivals to keep his presence and moving influence vividly in the minds of his worshippers.

It was curious to see the bazaars in the corridors and outer courts of the temple. Rows of stalls, where all sorts of miscellaneous things were sold—brass ware, pottery, woven stuffs, beads, and all kinds of knick-knacks and toys. Some of the sellers squat on the pavement and spread out their goods before them. The temple and its courts is a great resort of the people, in fact. Pilgrims lie down and sleep near its shrines, and the children play freely between its pillars. Bats flutter in and out of the crevices of the ceilings, or hang in little black clusters up aloft in their recesses.

In sketching at the sacred tank a very large crowd of natives gradually collected behind me, and on each side, and it was as much as the guide could do to keep them from closing in, and completely surrounding me. Some American visitors to the temple whom we met afterwards in Ceylon said that, seeing this vast concourse pressing round the tank, they thought it was a suicide! Travellers usually take snap-shots with hand cameras, and I imagine that a sketcher in colours is comparatively rare. The crowd, however, were quite quiet. The guide was encouraging, and remarked when I had finished that it was "better than a photograph."

Another afternoon we drove out through the city and some three miles beyond to see the "Teppa Tank"—a large sheet of water, enclosed by a low wall painted in red and white stripes, with steps to the water and carved bulls decorating the balustrades. On an island in the centre of the tank rose the pagoda of a temple, in stucco, and four small pagodas at the four corners of the garden-island—a mass of foliage amid which the pagodas shone, ivory-white in the sunshine.

Near this tank on the roadside was another temple sacred to a goddess who was the object of solicitude in the case of people desiring offspring, and to whom votive offerings of cradles were made by the devotees, as well as doll-like images of children made of baked clay and painted. The flat roof of this temple was peopled with a crowd of these grotesque images, and the carriage boy was sent to fetch one for our inspection.

Then we drove on to where grew a gigantic Banyan tree—eighty feet in girth, and having quite a small forest around its central vast trunk of offshoots—new trees which had rooted themselves in the earth from the parent branches. It was rather suggestive of a many pillared sylvan temple.

After this we reached the Palace of Tiramala,

which stood at the head of a large village—an imposing structure in stucco, mostly yellow washed. The enormous columns of the court looked out of proportion to the arches they supported, which were of a rather debased Mogul type, heavy with very elaborate grotesque ornamentation in stucco in the spandrils and on the ceilings, many of which had as a central device a large lotus flower formally treated as a rosette, and in some instances elaborately painted. The effect of the whole building was rather weird, and suggested a rather queer architectural nightmare, in which massive Norman cathedral piers had swallowed Roman Doric ones, or vice versa, and a Hindu modeller had broken up some Mogul arches, and fastened them together again with grotesque elephants and dragons' teeth.

The palace was now used as law courts, and it was curious to see two modern oil portraits of two neat English lawyers hanging on the walls of these vast columned halls.

We next visited a native shop in the village bazaar where the fine muslins and silks of the district were made and sold. We were duly seated in chairs and fanned by boys, while an active brown member of the firm unfolded tempting saris, pugarees, and silk stuffs, some beautifully brocaded with gold thread, and of course we possessed ourselves of a few specimens.

In this district there is a thriving native silk industry, hand-weaving, also dyeing, and the ingenious native craft of making patterns on cottons and muslins by tying and dipping. Hanks of cotton and silk may be seen hung out over bamboo poles placed horizontally, and ox carts roll by filled with the dyed skeins. There is a fine dark rich red, frequently seen in the sari dress of the women, also a dark purple. The women here generally wear the dark red sari with a narrow border of black; in some cases the sari is black with a red border.

In the village street we saw a little native bride drawn in a carriage.

Returning to the city in the cool of the evening we stopped at the temple bazaar and bought some zebu bells—curious little pear-shaped brass bells, each with a different tone, which are hung round the animals' necks. Their foreheads, too, are frequently bound with strings of beads, or shells fixed on leather bands, and their horns are painted green or red.

There is a method of decorating the centres of the dining tables in Southern India which, I think, we first noticed at the hotel at Madras, or at one of the refreshment stations on the Coromandel coast. It consists in arranging dyed sago seeds in patterns forming a table centre on the white cloth. At the station refreshment room at Madura there was a more elaborate example done by means of stencils—a border of yellow enclosed a lightly powdered filling, and an effective outer border was produced by a repeated sprig of a red rose with green leaves. The general effect was that of an embroidered pattern, but of course it was liable to slight displacements, and was constantly done afresh, one of the waiters being the special artist.

We left Madura on the 15th of February for Tuticorin.

The country traversed was flat and plain for the

TUTICORIN. DEPARTURE FOR COLOMBO. THE LAST OF THE KITES AND CROWS.

most part, with cultivated crops of castor oil plants, paddy, and corn, alternating with jungle of brushwood, but no fine trees. Hills were seen in the distance on the right, and we made several stoppages at short places with very long names.

Arriving at Tuticorin about four in the afternoon, we went on to the beach station, and got on board a small steam launch or tug in waiting at the jetty, then we saw the last quarter, as it were, of our Moon-sawmy, and took our leave of him, after he had had his usual fierce dispute with the coolies, who certainly never received trade union wages from *him.* On the whole we were not sorry to get away from the rupee-hunting throng, which usually hang about stations and wharves —the kites and crows in pursuit of the traveller, their prey, who for the time being, at least, now escaped their clutches.

Tuticorin presented no obvious attractions except the sea, which we were quite glad to meet again. The launch seemed just large enough to hold the train-load of passengers — Americans, Germans, and English with their baggage, and after about half-an-hour's steam across the harbour we reached the steamer (the "Pandua" of Glasgow) and climbed up the gangway to the saloon deck. We secured a rather small but well-appointed berth opening off the saloon, and were able to enjoy a well-served dinner—food seems generally better on ship-board than on land—at least Indian land. Cargo boats were clinging to the steamer's side, and, at sunset, one by one cast off and hoisted their lateen sails (like those of an Arab dhow) each boat having one about the length of the vessel. The sailors in hoisting up the sail climbed and clung to the rope, to bring it up with their weight.

Chanting a curious sort of song the while, our steamer weighed anchor and started, and we looked astern and saw the last of India fading from view behind the shining wake of the steamer, and lost in the glow of an orange sunset.

CHAPTER XV

NOTES OF CEYLON

THE voyage across the straits to Colombo proved to be wonderfully calm, which was rather unusual as we understood it was as a rule tempestuous, and we did not find our cabin nearly so hot as our room at Madura. We sighted the coast of Ceylon early in the morning of February 16, and got into harbour at Colombo about 8 A.M. A fleet of fishing boats had previously passed us, of the curious native rig—a square sail apparently arranged to sail before the wind only. Our steamer was soon surrounded by a little fleet of odd shaped outrigger canoes, some of them mere planks, paddled by active little darkie boys, who dived for small silver coins if they could induce the passengers to throw them. These little amphibians seemed as much at home in the water as in their canoes, and they swam like fishes.

Our good friend Mr Bois sent a messenger on board to meet us and help us through the customs, having secured us rooms at the Galle Face. Most things are chargeable under the tariff, but the traveller pays duty on his own valuation.

The steamer did not land its passengers at the quay, but anchored in the harbour, and everyone landed in boats. The Hotel boats, manned by native oarsmen, row swiftly to the Custom House, and often race each other. After passing the customs we got into a little Victoria and drove straight to the Galle Face.

Not much can be said for the architectural

LANDING AT COLOMBO

beauty of Colombo, the buildings being, generally speaking, of ordinary commercial type. The Grand Oriental Hotel, or G.O.H. as it is commonly called, is a big pile near the harbour, and has an arcade surrounding the ground story, like most of the stores, and continuous balconies above, partitioned off according to the rooms which open on to them. Here and there there is a relic of the Dutch occupation in some of the frontages with round recessed arches and pilasters.

The Governor's house, as usual, is the most attractive looking building, half hidden amidst masses of palms and other trees. A rather bold clock tower faces a long esplanade, which extends for nearly half a mile along the sea front, at the end of which is situated the Galle Face Hotel, with its cluster of slender-stemmed cocoa palms leaning over the sea. Here, the long ocean breakers rolling in, the turquoise waves melting into dazzling foam, seen through the palm trees has an enchanting effect, both in the sunlight and the moonlight. There was a young crescent at night—seen, as only seen in the East, on its back—floating like a fairy boat, and casting a mysterious light over the dark ocean, the waving palms overhead and the sound of the breaking waves adding to the wonderful charm of the scene.

Jin-rickshaws were in great request, but the supply seemed fully equal to the demand, and the esplanade was always full of the trotting boys drawing white clad Europeans in topis up and down the terra-cotta coloured road. There was a wide, green strip extending along the drive, and on the other side of the suburbs of Colombo extended northwards, chiefly native houses, and bungalows of European residents often enclosed in gardens and hidden in ample foliage of trees.

The hotel was served by an army of Cingalese waiters who wore their hair much like the southern Indians—long, like a woman's, and done up in a

UNDER THE PALMS AT THE GALLE FACE, CEYLON

knot at the back, their peculiar distinction, however, being a semicircular comb of tortoise-shell worn like a coronet on the top of the head, but with the

COMMON OBJECTS OF COLOMBO. (JIN-RICKSHAWUS BIPEDES)

open points in front. Otherwise their costume consisted of a close white skirt, and a neat white jacket with green facings. Their feet were always bare, like the Indian boys.

There was a band at dinner, served in a vast white hall, and after, on the terrace, when the guests would sit out among the palms lighted up by jewels of electric light. The white breakers foaming under the moon, the shadowy waving

A CINGALESE WAITER

palms, the sky flashing with sheet lightning, the brilliantly lighted hotel, and the white figures flitting about "among the guests star-scattered on the grass," all contributed to a striking stage effect.

The hotel was certainly spacious and well appointed, having large cool corridors and rooms to sit in—comparatively cool that is to say, and without the gloom of so many of the Indian hotels. In the matter of food, cookery, and the service too, it was a great improvement on the Peninsula. There were electric fans everywhere in motion, and we could always turn one on in our room—which was normally an oven. The draft from these fans, however, are said to be apt to give people chills, and some caution in their use in bed-rooms is necessary.

We visited our friends in their charming house—one of the older style of Colombo dwellings, in a delightful garden where afternoon-tea was served on a pleasant lawn shaded by fine trees, among which we recognised the forest flame, which with its wonderful scarlet blossoms had struck us on the way to Darjeeling, though not then in flower here.

Another day Mr Bois took us out for a drive in his motor all around Colombo and its neighbourhood. We went through the town and along by the dry dock, and through the native quarter (Zeppa or Teppa) and away through narrow lanes shaded by cocoa palms, plantains, banyans, mangoes and other trees growing with tropical luxuriance each side the way, in plantations, and around the bungalows.

The motor seemed a strange vehicle in the midst of the primitive life of the Cingalese; and it is said that extremes meet, and certainly a motor and a primitive ox-wagon represent about the greatest contrast in means of locomotion and transport that one can well imagine. It was rather wonderful that we escaped a collision sometimes meeting such vehicles in the narrow lanes, or that we avoided running over stray chickens or dogs—the latter kind always resenting the motor and imperilling

IN CEYLON—EXTREMES MEET—THE MOTOR AND THE OX-CART

their lives by running and barking in close proximity with the enemy. The natives we met walking, too, were by no means alert in getting out of the way, and did not seem to realise the danger.

We passed mission houses and churches of all sorts, and of every shade of theological colour—Wesleyans, Roman Catholics, and Salvation Army—all the plagues of sectarian Christianity which afflict humanity in Europe, alas!

Our friend said, à propos of some remarks of mine about the ignorance and indifference of missionaries as to native religions and their natural suitability to the races, and their habits of life and the climates where they are found, that he had cautioned missionaries against running down the native religion. This in Ceylon, is mainly Buddhist (and Buddha surely discovered something analogous to Christian ethics, if not superior, long before Christ). The Tamils are Buddhists, but there are some Hindus and Mohammedans in Ceylon, and even pure Buddhism is mingled in some curious way with a primitive devil-worship.

We saw the golf links and a golf club house—quite *à la Anglaise*—on a rising ground and bare of trees, for a wonder in Ceylon. It appeared that these links occupied the site of a farm which did not succeed. Then we saw the river, where an engineer's iron bridge had taken the place of a former bridge of boats. Colombo must have largely lost its primitive and Dutch character when the old Fort was destroyed. This has been replaced by terribly ugly Barrack buildings, and the town is rapidly becoming a modern commercial centre, big warehouses and universal provider's stores are rising up after the European or American type. The native character, however, manifests itself still, peeping out here and there, especially in the older shops, and there is more native costume to be seen than one had imagined. The country ox-cart is a striking object with its huge tilt of matting projecting forward and backward like a hood, the single zebu by which it is usually drawn appearing small for the size of the vehicle.

We did not see many native women about, but those we did see wore the native dress, consisting of a white bodice, cut round and rather low in the neck, with a lace edging; a necklace and earrings, and the narrow skirt wrapped about the lower half of the figure to the feet generally printed with a pattern, or chequered, similar to that worn by the men.

We drove round by the Cinnamon gardens, and rested at a club house—a mixed European Club—a pleasant house with a large and well-kept croquet lawn in front where ladies were playing. We sat a while, after being refreshed and making some new acquaintances, we returned in the motor to our hotel.

We had thunder and lightning at night. The lightning flashing almost incessantly all over the heavens, but mostly from great clouds rolling up from the north and east.

While sitting at tea in the hall of the Galle Face one afternoon we met an old friend in the person of Mr Cyril Holman Hunt, the son of the famous pre-Raphaelite painter, who had been a planter for some years, first in Ceylon and afterwards in the Straits, from which he had just arrived. So that it was quite a chance our meeting, as he was not even staying at the same hotel.

The same evening the officers of the Italian warship *Marco Polo* were entertained at dinner at the Galle Face, and their band played selections afterwards.

The scene in the hall of a Colombo hotel is always busy, but in a different way to a European hostelry—one might almost say it was feverish haste in the midst of languid indolence—a ballet of energetic action before a crowd of unconcerned spectators. While some are in the fuss of departure or arrival, rows of enervated travellers lounge in wicker chairs, reading, chatting, smoking, or engaged with tea or cooling drinks, mostly attired in white; many of the ladies in delicate summer dresses, the men in white drill or tussore suits. All nationalities are represented, the majority American, and mostly people waiting for their steamers outward or homeward.

Most visitors to Ceylon make a trip to Kandy, and one morning early saw us on our way thither. The railway carriages are good and comfortable, but they do not allow the stacking of hand luggage in them as they do to such an extent on the Indian railways. The train passed through a very rich and fruitful-looking country, where the paddy crops in different stages—under water, green and ripe or being reaped and thrashed—reminded us of India. The fields were generally surrounded by groves of plantains and palms.

The vegetation being most luxuriant everywhere. banyans, mangoes, and flowering trees of different kinds including spireas and the "forest flame" we saw at Darjeeling ; tangled masses of creepers hanging from the boughs, and often covering the whole tree. Several rivers were crossed the red earth showing on their banks, and the water generally tinged with the same.

We reached Kandy about 11.15, the train ascending to this place about 4400 feet. The line curving up the slopes so that we could frequently see the engine and forepart of the train rounding the loop in front of us. We could only secure a room for one night at the hotel (the Queen's), so that we had to make the most of our time. Accordingly, after tiffin, we started in a carriage for what the hotel people prosaically called "No. 2. drive" (!).

Skirting the large tank or lake in front of the hotel, which has a solid stone palisading around it cut into points and pierced, we ascended a steep road, winding up the hills through lovely woodlands, at every turn presenting fine mountainous and panoramic views of the country. Beautiful clusters of bamboo of enormous size occurred frequently, the stems very thick and of an oxidized bronze colour, varying from dark to light. Another kind had bright golden coloured stems, and a lighter, more feathery foliage. Cocoa palms, plantains, and mangoes were abundant, also cinnamon plants. A native boy offered us a cocoa bean pod, and a spray of cinnamon— a pretty tree with a tassel-like flower. There were also large trees bearing massive pendulous fruits, which grow directly out of the trunk suspended on very short stalks in clusters of two and three. This fruit was called "Jack fruit." It looked like a sort of gigantic walnut, and was covered with a soft green velvety kind of rind. The leaves of this tree was small and poplar-like in shape. The brilliant scarlet lily-like bloom of a dark leaved shrub was often seen, the flower having long stamens hanging out like a tassel.

The various drives which had been made over the hills and through these great woods were apparently named after different governors' wives. There was Lady Longden's drive, Lady Macarthy's, Lady Horton's, and so on. We sometimes had the impression, as the carriage followed the gravelled curves of these drives, that we were approaching some country seat among the hills. The drives, though well planned for points of view, and well kept, were, perhaps, a little too suggestive of the landscape gardener, a little too conscious and laid out to order, to be thoroughly enjoyable. We should have preferred to see the untouched work of the original designer of Ceylon scenery. The natural wild country unanglicised—though I know I should be told that without such roads and clearings one would not be able to see the country at all.

We British, somehow, always seem to carry suburban ideas with us everywhere, and English trimness and neatness even out into the tropical wilderness: We passed neat homes surrounded by smooth tennis and croquet lawns, as if bits of Chiselhurst or Surbiton had been suddenly dumped down in the midst of all this wonderful world of luxuriant growth and unfamiliar trees, and close to native huts of the most primitive kind.

The native roof here, as at Darjeeling, appeared

to be èither thatch or wooden shingles, and here, again, we were sorry to see corrugated iron creep-into use everywhere.

The most primæval sight we had was perhaps that of the elephants bathing in the river. This was at a spot close to a native village, where we left our carriage and, walking through a grove, came out on the river shore where five or six black elephants—one a large one with fine tusks—were disporting themselves in the water, in charge of native attendants, rolling over on their sides and squirting the water over themselves by means of their trunks with the greatest enjoyment. The water was rather thick and reddish in colour from the clay of the banks.

On the way back to the hotel we passed the famous Buddhist Temple of the Tooth with its pagoda-like roof, but it looks but an insignificant building to be the centre of Buddhistic reverence and tribute.

This was a lovely moonlight night, and the walk by the lake would have been perfect but for the touts and vendors of all sorts of things that you do not want.

We left Kandy the next morning for Nuwara-Eliya our travelling companions were two Germans from Berlin, father and son. The train continued to climb, the line curving more sharply than before. We saw some fine mountain distances and Adam's Peak rising up afar, and soon entered a vast tea-planted district the tea plants often bordering the railway line, and covering the slopes of the hills which seemed covered with a more or less regular green pattern, the dark velvety green of the tea plants intersected by the light feathery foliage of young rubber-trees, planted in regular rows at intervals in some places. The landscape was very

TEA PLANTATION, CEYLON

"She liked coffee, and I liked tea,
And that is the reason we always agree!"

clear and every detail sharply defined in the bright sunlight, with very little suggestion of atmosphere, except for the mountain distances which were deep blue.

In the afternoon about four or five o'clock we reached Nunnoya station, where we had to change into a narrow-gauge train to finish the last part of the journey to Nuwara-Eliya. We continued to climb in shorter and more loop-like curves, being able often to gaze down on the line we had just traversed winding below like a glittering serpent among the wooded hills and tea plantations. Tea everywhere, and not a drop to drink—yet suggesting potentially more than the whole world could consume.

Something after five found us at Nuwara-Eliya where we got into a wagonette, and a good pair of greys brought us through the village to the St Andrews Hotel, a very pleasant homelike place in a nice garden and backed by beautiful woods. The original house looked as if it might have been a private residence, and there was just a touch of Rydal Mount about it and its situation, at the first glance, but a new wing had been added with a tin-roof, and there was a golf course in the valley just below.

The valley is very beautiful, with its richly wooded hills and a lake with blue mountainous distance. Delicate feathery, aspen-like trees wave in the soft air, and there are numbers of firs and cypresses which give an Italian touch to the landscape, but no palms. In fact, the whole character of the country is totally different from Colombo and Kandy. The climate, too, is much cooler, the thermometer falling to 40 degrees at night, or even to frost, though the sun is hot enough in the middle of the day.

There is a native bazaar, and an English quarter with a red club house, tennis courts, and a race-course—of course. St Andrews, however, where we were quartered, was quite away by itself, and was altogether perhaps the pleasantest place we had stayed at either in India or Ceylon. It was possible, for one thing, to walk out without being worried by guides and touts, or to buy things. The climate was delightful after the enervating heat of Colombo, and there being hardly any other guests the quiet of the place was a great relief and very restful.

One afternoon we had a walk up the opposite hills, the track being mostly through tea-plantations, with forest bits occasionally. The tea tree left to itself apparently grows high on a stem, having a very striking character and shape, suggesting almost the stone-pine. The small, thick-stemmed, closely-trimmed, flat-headed dwarf bushes which are its characteristic forms in the tea plantations also have an interesting effect in some situations on the hill-sides, intersected by wandering paths whereon the dark natives move up and down. The tea-plant has a leaf somewhat of the character of a laurel or orange tree, and its flower recalls that of the orange. Ceylon tea when made is of a beautiful clear orange colour—I mean when poured from the pot.

The Hagdalla gardens, founded by the government in 1861, well repay a visit, and are deeply interesting to anyone interested in the flora of Ceylon. It is a drive of about six miles; passing through the native village, and by the English Club and race-course, the lake is skirted, and after that the road takes the character rather of a mountain pass, and runs along the edge of a deep wooded ravine down which a rocky stream tumbles into falls over boulders. There was just a touch of a sort of Borrowdale, translated into Cingalee, about this part of the drive. The wild forest which clad the hills each side of the valley was very different in character and colour to anything seen in Europe, the trees showed the most lovely tints of varied bronze, from pale green to copper red. The tea tree was abundant, and the rhododendron, which here is totally different in character and general shape to the cultivated shrub-like bushes in English gardens. Here it is a thick-stemmed tree, with a rugged bark, and a bold irregular outline with rather sparse leavage and deep crimson flowers which glow splendidly among the dark metallic green of the leaves. There is a sort of formal grotesqueness about the tree, too, which is rather Chinese.

On the way through the ravine, at a solitary spot below the road, we saw a Buddhist shrine. On a little platform surrounded by a rough fence of loose stones, and facing the road, was a row of carved images, in some dark wood, standing figures of Buddha. In front of this rude structure we saw a native worshipper prostrating himself on the edge of the road, and bowing and bending towards the shrine.

The Magdalla gardens are botanic and horticultural gardens laid out with great care and skill on the slope of a mountain. They apparently contain all the varieties of trees and plants indigenous to Ceylon. Tree ferns are there in abundance, flowering trees of many kinds, and parasitic plants, and orchids in great variety, growing in their natural manner. As one threads the narrow wandering paths it is as if one passed through a thick jungle or tropical forest, only that the walking is made easy, and botanical labels here and there, and signs of gardener's care and labour, remind one it is a garden.

There is a keeper's lodge, in this Cingalese paradise, covered with creepers, and a formal level parterre in front, one mass of brilliant floral colour —African marigolds, fuchsias, poppies, *blue* centred daisies, sunflowers, blue convolvulus, Amaryllis, and white eucharis lilies, canaryensis, polyanthus and many more; some that might be found in English gardens and hot-houses, with other tropical wonders only seen at Kew.

After a ramble here we returned to the carriage, and drove back through the now burning sun.

Gorse grows about the links and open common-like ground in the valley at Nuwara-Eliya, though the bushes seem to grow rather taller and straighter than they do in England. Instead of our lords and ladies, arum lilies grow wild. Great clusters of them may be seen by the sides of streams or in marshy places. The woods were delightful to wander in, and altogether Nuwara-Eliya might make good claims to be an earthly paradise, other things being equal.

We had taken our passage, however, from Colombo, and were due to sail for home on the 2nd of March. It was now the 28th of February, and we had to make our way back again, descending from Il Paradiso to a certainly hotter region. The descent by the narrow gauge railway was even more striking than the ascent, the train passing through luxuriant growths of forest in which tree-ferns, rhododendrons, the tea tree, and what looked like a sort of box tree were abundant.

The rubber-trade in Ceylon is now being added to the tree-trade, which, according to our competitive wasteful individualistic system, has somewhat outgrown its profitable market. One effect of this new development upon the landscape is devastation, as large tracts of wild forest on the mountain sides are being cleared by burning the natural growth in the first place, and then removing the stones and boulders which cumber the ground. This process does not add to the beauty of the scenery, nor can we expect that monotonous plantations will be good substitutes to the eye for the wild beauty and varied and luxuriant vegetation they displace.

The Englishman in Ceylon seems to think of nothing but profit-making, however, like many of his race elsewhere; and is probably often even unaware of the beauty he destroys for commercial reasons, and he is always able to import cheap coolie labour from India to carry out his schemes.

The Cingalese native it seems is unwilling to work, or probably has not the physique for heavy field labour, so he prefers to live the natural life of his country so far as he is allowed by his new masters, and of course is denounced as a lazy dog.

Ceylon, indeed, one cannot help reflecting must have been a delightful paradise, if somewhat warm in parts, for its own people, before they were interfered with by western civilisation, with its pushful commerce, and missions, bringing in their train poverty and disease, and the struggle for existence, in a land naturally fruitful and bountiful, and able to support its inhabitants without any special efforts on their part.

The planters are now clamouring for railway

TEA AND RUBBER IN CEYLON—A RISING INDUSTRY

extension. In an interview which the Editor of *The Ceylon Times* sought with me I gathered that there was considerable discontent with the Home Government, who, he asserted, had derived greatly increased revenues from the extension of rubber planting and the new development of the industry, but who would not grant money for the desired extensions, the advice given by the present secretary for the colonies being to the effect that the Ceylon people should save their money, or "put by for a rainy day."

Of course the Editor's point of view was that of the capitalist, and that the more the country was opened up the better, and he did not care to consider the effects of the ultimate outcome of the monolopy which absorbs the results of and succeeds commercial competition.

He spoke, however, incidentally of the increase of poverty—poverty in such a land!—and that there was no poor law *yet.* He said the Cingalese would not work, and had even neglected the irrigation machinery which had been set up by the planters for their benefit, *in obedience to the requirements of the home government.*

This would seem to show the difficulty of introducing ostensible benefits in a primitive country which has not reached the necessary stage of development to be able to take advantage of, or really to utilise, modern methods. From the point of view of the simple native no doubt there does not appear to be any reason why he should change the habits and customs of his race simply for the benefit of foreign settlers whose chief object is to exploit him.

Changing trains at Nunnoya we were again greatly impressed by the splendour of the scenery traversed. For a great part of the distance towards Kandy and Colombo, the line passes through a mountainous district, at a high altitude, gradually descending, the line following the contours of the hill-sides for the most part, though tunnelled occasionally. One looks across a wide valley with distant mountain ranges, ridge beyond ridge, in marked and emphatic outlines, and occasionally abrupt precipices—the sharp conical summit of Adam's Peak conspicuous among them. The hill-sides are largely covered with tea-plantations, but the railway also passes through wild bush and forest, and high above one may see great towering crags of limestone and gritstone. Mountain streams are frequently crossed, and these break into cascades and falls among tumbled black rocks; great boulders frequently strew the mountain slopes as if tumbled by Titans among the foliage. There is occasionally a suggestion of Derbyshire scenery here and there, but on a grander scale.

After Kandy the line descends still more till we reach the palm groves again, the river, and the lakes, and the heat of Colombo again. This time on returning we put up at the G.O.H., which is conveniently near the pier or departure stage for the steamers.

Here we met Mr Cyril Holman Hunt again, and were introduced to several of his planter friends, who were very agreeable. There is a delightful garden of palms and tropical plants here, which is a pleasant resort in the cool of the evenings. With Mr Hunt we visited the Colombo Museum, which was courteously opened specially for us, it not being a public day. Here in a glass case and alive some extraordinary leaf-insects arrested our attention. They were feeding on green leaves, which they exactly resembled in colour, form, and texture, so that it would be most difficult to tell which was leaf and which was insect without closely watching them. The young ones were like the red shoots of a plant, but the mature insects were quite green and quite flat like a leaf while showing the ribs and veinings. One could hardly have believed that nature, deceptive and imitative as she is, could have been capable of such a trick. I remember that a native at Kandy had shown me one of the green leaf insects in a box, but I thought it was an artificial thing, which indeed it looks.

On the staircase were some copies of exceedingly interesting ancient Cingalese fresco-paintings from caves, resembling ancient Indian work in style, but in some instances showing a certain freedom in handling, the brush outline recalling later Greek vase-painting.

There were excellent collections of native Cingalese decorative art in jewellery, silver work, and ivory-carving, of which latter craft some combs were the most delicate and interesting. There were also block-printed stuffs similar to the Indian hand-printed cottons. Among the jewellery, the necklaces of garnets and other stones set in filagree gold were characteristic. There were models of native boats of which there are several interesting varieties, and these were exceptionally good life-sized models of types of the aboriginal inhabitants (the Veddas)—the wild bush-tribes of Ceylon.

The natural history department was very complete, and the whole museum judiciously comprehended the history, natural and archæological, of the island, and included some highly interesting Greco-Buddhistic sculptured remains, not so fine in style as those we had seen at Sarnath, but there was the same type of standing figure in drapery expressing the lines of the figure, and also portions of an "umbrella," showing a similar arrangement to the one at Sarnath, with the lotus flower centre, and the series of concentric rings of ornament containing the images of the lion, the horse, the ox, and the elephant in sunk relief. There was also a zoological collection attached to the museum in sheds and aviaries outside the main building—live animals and birds, including leopards, jackals, monkeys, flamingoes, pelicans, and a collection of small birds, minas, doves, etc.

The time, however, for our departure from Colombo drew near. Our steamer the *Tourane* of the Messageries Maritime line arrived punctually on March the 2nd, calling at Colombo on her homeward voyage from China, and the same evening saw us aboard.

We made our adieus, and our steamer cast off, or rather weighed anchor, about sunset, and we were soon under way. The dinner-bell rang at 6.30, and going on deck afterwards we saw the last of Colombo—a mere thread of glittering beads of light on the horizon, and soon lost in the darkness of night.

There was a large proportion of French people among the passengers, and they were chiefly officials and their families returning on leave from Chinese stations. They were exceedingly gay and lively, and always had plenty of conversation. It was like a continual comedy going on with much variety of character.

On the 7th day, after a voyage of undisturbed

serenity over the Indian ocean, the blueness of the sea varied only by the steamer's track, and the foam dancing into rainbows, with flying fish, or an occasional turtle, or an albatross or two, which flapped heavily after us, we sighted Aden, and rounded the striking rocky coast to cast anchor off the port. Here the tugs brought up the coal lighters, and the cargo boats, and the swarm of Soumalis, as before, and the usual bazaar on deck took place, and the hauling of the coal and cargo went on all through the night—the clamours of the coolies being occasionally fiendish, and the din was often punctuated by bangs on an iron bar, which sent a shiver through the ship. This was the method of giving warning to the man engaged in the loading operations in the hold. We afterwards learned that two poor coolies had lost their lives by venturing into the hold before it had been ventilated, and the air was so foul as to suffocate them, and a ship's officer who went to their rescue also became insensible for a time. It seemed much hotter, too, now the ship was stationary.

Artillery practice was going on from the fort the next morning, and we could see the shots strike the water. We did not get clear of Aden till about 10 A.M., but at last the swarm of boats and swarthy Soumalis left us, and the *Tourane* entered on her course through the Red Sea, and in due time passed Mocha (to starboard) and Perim (to port) and the Arabian coast, the sea churned into foam by the steamer flashed with phosphorescence at night,—the effect in the wake of the vessel being very beautiful, green sparks appearing and floating on the surface, and globes of subdued light glowed under the fleeting foam, rapidly swept along and lost in the darkness of the night lit only by stars—among which the Great Bear showed how much we had altered our latitude.

The heat continued very great for three days after leaving Aden, when it rather suddenly grew cooler, and by the time we passed "the Brothers" towards evening on the 12th of March, the weather grew quite grey and cloudy with a cold wind.

We reached Suez early on the morning of the 13th, and here it was fine and bright again, though the air felt thin and cool. The colour of the water had changed, too, and was now a fine clear turquoise—precisely the colour of the Egyptian glass bracelets, but dark blue on the horizon and against the land, which looked pink.

The drama of the official tug and the cargo boats was again performed, and there was much hoisting of coffee-bags, in and out, and a taking of fresh provisions on board. The Traders came aboard, too, with Fez caps, bead and shell necklaces, post-cards, and other trifles. It was amusing to see our French friends buying the Fez freely, and not only wearing them themselves but putting them on the heads of their children. There had already been some astonishing transformations in costume on board since the cooler weather set in, topis and white drill being exchanged for tweed suits and caps or felt hats, and, in some cases, smart official uniforms with shakos.

We left Suez about the middle of the day and entered the canal, the water still such a brilliant turquoise colour that the reflection in the strong sunlight caused the white breasts of the sea-gulls, which now followed our ship, to appear green.

A FEW TRIFLES THE WIFE WISHED TO BRING HOME FROM INDIA

We made some very agreeable acquaintances on board, which made the time pass more quickly, and we arrived at Port Said early on Friday the 14th of March. The coaling *this* time was a comparatively clean process, the wind not being ahead as before. Some few of the passengers got off for

Egypt here, but we were soon under way again; and M. de Lèsseps' large effigy, the green dome of the Custom House, the steamers, the wharves, and the posters of Port Said soon all faded from view as we bade farewell to the East and entered the Mediterranean on our way to Marseilles, the last stage of our long voyage, where after some tossing we had a passing vision of snow-capped Sicily, and the Lipari Islands, with Stromboli still smoking away; and so, in due course, through the straits of Bonifazio, with no further sea troubles, landed at Marseilles on March 19, safe and sound.

INDEX